5

INGREDIENT
SEMI-HOMEMADE
Meals

by *flavcity*

5 INGREDIENT SEMI-HOMEMADE *Meals*

by *flavcity*

50 Easy & Tasty Recipes Using
the Best Ingredients
from the Grocery Store

BOBBY PARRISH AND DESSI PARRISH

mango
PUBLISHING GROUP

CORAL GABLES

5 Ingredient Semi-Homemade Meals by FlavCity: 50 Easy & Tasty Recipes
Using the Best Ingredients from the Grocery Store

Library of Congress Cataloging-in-Publication number: 2020945248
ISBN: (print) 978-1-64250-484-2, (ebook) 978-1-64250-485-9
BISAC Category Code CKB113000, COOKING /
Methods / Low Budget

Printed in the United States of America

This book is
dedicated to the millions
of FlavCity fans
around the world!

CONTENTS

Writing a cookbook with Rose attached to our hip the entire time was a bit challenging, but I would not trade it for anything! While taking photos, Rose would either be in my arms, shaking the table, or pulling down the lights. She's my favorite ingredient and here's the best photo in the book!

INTRODUCTION

Raise your hand if you spend too much time in the grocery store staring at the wall of pastas, condiments, and cooking oils wondering which ones are the best. This cookbook is for you. It contains all my shopping knowledge along with over fifty epic recipes that use the best ingredients and products from the grocery store. Grocery shopping and cooking are my two big passions in life. If you follow me @flavcity on social media, you know this. So I thought it would be fun to not only teach you how to cook really easy and tasty meals using five ingredients, but also how to navigate the grocery store and choose the best items to cook with.

It amazes me how much garbage is out there! I mean, seriously—have you read the ingredients on some of these products? And how many of them are in your pantry and fridge right now? I'm going to school you on every single aisle in the grocery store and help you locate the major ingredient offenders to stay away from. Spoiler alert! These ingredients are in the majority of items from the middle aisles of the store. You're also going to learn how to take some truly amazing products that have best-in-class ingredients and make super easy and healthy recipes at home. These recipes are easy enough that anyone can make them. Yes, everyone. That was the reason I wanted to write this book. I believe the key to overall health is cooking your own meals and knowing exactly what goes into your body, along with a few workouts per week; if you do that, nothing can stop you!

I really think this book is one of a kind, combing expert shopping tips that I have learned while making hundreds of grocery haul videos on the *FlavCity* YouTube channel along with recipes that have monster flavor with minimal ingredients and effort.

We just launched the Bobby Approved app. I highly suggest giving it a try. It has all of my shopping knowledge, a detailed breakdown of every aisle in the store, and a bar code scanner that tells you if a product is Bobby Approved. Search for the app in the App Store and Google Play Store.

QUICK REFERENCE ICONS:

KETO
—

Indicates recipe
is **Ketogenic**
diet compliant

PALEO
—

Indicates recipe is **Paleo**
diet compliant

VEGAN
—

Indicates recipe is **Vegan**
diet compliant

—

No Gluten
(indicates recipes
contains
no gluten)

—

No Eggs
(indicates recipes
contains no eggs)

—

No Dairy
(indicates recipes
contains no dairy)

—

No Nuts
(indicates recipes
contains no nuts)

—

Video Tutorial
(indicates there's
a video tutorial
on YouTube for
this recipe)

Shopping Tip

—

Shopping Tip

PANTRY

—

**Pantry Staple
Ingredient**

—

**Wish List
Ingredient**

FLAVCITY CHANGED THE WAY I READ LABELS! I DREADED

READING LABELS BEFORE. I NEVER PAID ATTENTION

TO THE ADDED SUGARS, NATURAL FLAVORS, OR TYPES

OF OILS, AND DIDN'T UNDERSTAND WHAT EXPELLER

PRESSED MEANT! THANKS TO FLAVCITY, READING

LABELS IS MUCH EASIER NOW AND TAKES LESS TIME.

–MARIAM A.

HOW TO NAVIGATE THE GROCERY STORE LIKE A BOSS

This book is loaded with shopping tips that will change the way you navigate the grocery store. Here are some general shopping guidelines before you get into recipes and detailed grocery tips. Keep in mind, I have hundreds of grocery haul videos on YouTube, including hauls from Costco, ALDI, Trader Joe's, Whole Foods, Walmart and more! If you ever have a question, search "FlavCity + XYZ" on YouTube.

Beef:

When it comes to beef, 100% grass fed is the way to go. Otherwise, the cattle eat a strict diet of GMO corn and soy. The nutritional profile of grass-fed beef is far superior to grain-fed, plus it's better for the environment, farmer, cows, and you. 100% grass fed is the same as grass fed and grass finished. If the label does not say one of those two terms, put it back. That means it was finished on grain and that defeats the whole point.

Chicken:

Always buy organic chicken and turkey. Better yet, it would be pasture raised, but you can't find that at the grocery store yet. Organic means the chickens are fed non-GMO grain, but the beauty of pasture raised is that the chickens are outside all day, not in a hen house, and the nutritional profile is much better. Find pasture-raised chicken at eatwild.com by searching using your zip code.

Pork:

Pasture-raised pork is unlike anything you have ever tried from the grocery store! The flavor and texture are lights-out and they don't stay inside eating GMO grains all day. Unfortunately, you can't find this at grocery stores. Search for local farms using your zip code at eatwild.com.

Shrimp:

Always go for wild-caught USA and Mexican shrimp. The farming practices for shrimp have a bad reputation, especially in Asia, and we have a bounty of wild-caught shrimp in this country.

Farm-Raised Salmon:

Farm-raised salmon gets a bad reputation. That's because there are lots of farms around the world doing it the wrong way. Overcrowded pens and low-quality feed—these are just a few cut corners when it comes to farm-raised salmon. I will teach you how to select the best-quality farmed salmon and why it's actually better for some recipes because it's so fatty, making it very hard to overcook. Search "FlavCity seafood buying guide" on YouTube to learn lots more.

Wild-Caught Salmon:

Wild-caught salmon is readily available these days, just make sure it's caught and processed in the USA. You would be surprised how much salmon is outsourced to China for processing. My only issue is that most wild-caught salmon is very lean and easy to overcook. That's why I tend to make salmon cakes and burgers with it. You will learn more about that in the seafood chapter.

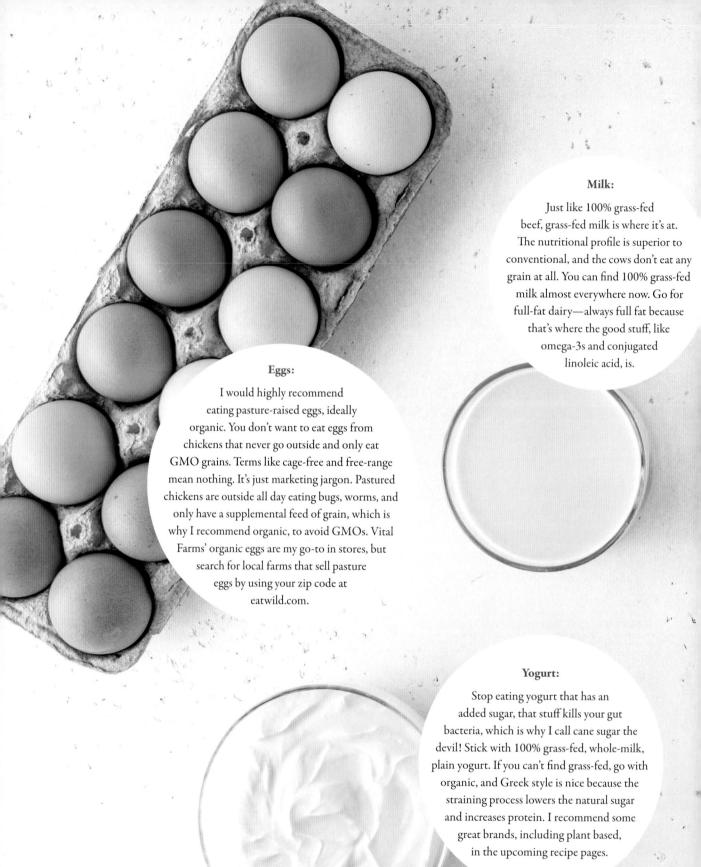

Milk:

Just like 100% grass-fed beef, grass-fed milk is where it's at. The nutritional profile is superior to conventional, and the cows don't eat any grain at all. You can find 100% grass-fed milk almost everywhere now. Go for full-fat dairy—always full fat because that's where the good stuff, like omega-3s and conjugated linoleic acid, is.

Eggs:

I would highly recommend eating pasture-raised eggs, ideally organic. You don't want to eat eggs from chickens that never go outside and only eat GMO grains. Terms like cage-free and free-range mean nothing. It's just marketing jargon. Pastured chickens are outside all day eating bugs, worms, and only have a supplemental feed of grain, which is why I recommend organic, to avoid GMOs. Vital Farms' organic eggs are my go-to in stores, but search for local farms that sell pasture eggs by using your zip code at eatwild.com.

Yogurt:

Stop eating yogurt that has an added sugar, that stuff kills your gut bacteria, which is why I call cane sugar the devil! Stick with 100% grass-fed, whole-milk, plain yogurt. If you can't find grass-fed, go with organic, and Greek style is nice because the straining process lowers the natural sugar and increases protein. I recommend some great brands, including plant based, in the upcoming recipe pages.

Butter:

I always go for Kerrygold or Organic Valley cultured butter. It's a bit tougher to find 100% grass-fed butter, but these are two of the best options in the dairy section.

Cheese:

Same rule applies here, look for 100% grass-fed, or at least organic. I would never buy pre-grated cheese. They are loaded with anti-caking agents. Plus, they don't melt as well compared to grating it yourself. If you can find raw and 100% grass-fed cheese, that is the absolute best you can do. And guess what? I will show you how to find it!

THE MIDDLE AISLES

This is the scariest part of the grocery store—prepackaged foods, sauces, snacks, breads, and more, loaded with inflammatory plant-based oils, nasty preservatives, added sugar, artificial flavors, gluten, and more. But once you learn how to shop, which I will teach you, you will be able to avoid all that stuff and focus on the Bobby Approved products that are made with best-in-class ingredients.

THIS BOOK IS 100% GLUTEN FREE

Not because I'm allergic, it's because gluten is inflammatory, and we keep a keto and paleo house for the most part. If you want the best bread at the store, go for organic and sprouted bread. Search "FlavCity bread" on YouTube to learn lots more! There are lots of garbage gluten-free products at the store. I will show you how to choose the best-quality, most nutrient-dense items.

PROCESSED OILS

Stay away from any product that uses canola, soybean, corn, sunflower, or safflower oil. These are highly processed oils that are usually made from GMO crops and are very inflammatory. The problem is most ready-bought items use these oils, and the reason is because they are cheap! You will notice that I only cook with avocado, virgin coconut, and olive oil, and the Bobby Approved products used for these recipes contain only the best oils and other ingredients. Search "FlavCity cooking oil" on YouTube for lots more information.

CANE SUGAR IS THE DEVIL!

It not only makes us fat, but it also kills good gut bacteria and is inflammatory. It's amazing what happens to your body when you stop eating sugar along with other inflammatory foods. You start to lose weight and feel great! I have a fantastic video about the most inflammatory foods at the store. Search "FlavCity inflammation" on YouTube. There are incredible paleo sweeteners like maple syrup and honey, and keto sweeteners like monk fruit. These are the types of sweeteners we use in this book and what you want to have in your pantry. Search "FlavCity sweeteners" on YouTube. These videos have loads of information.

PRODUCE

I highly advise you to buy organic produce when it comes to the dirty dozen. These fruits and veggies are some of the most highly sprayed crops and scary levels of chemicals persist even after washing them!

(Check out EWG.com, they have excellent information of this topic.)

DIRTY DOZEN PLUS ONE

1. STRAWBERRIES

2. SPINACH

3. KALE

4. NECTARINES

5. APPLES

6. GRAPES

7. PEACHES

8. CHERRIES

9. PEARS

10. TOMATOES

11. CELERY

12. POTATOES

13. SWEET BELL PEPPERS

CLEAN FIFTEEN

1. AVOCADOS

2. PINEAPPLES

3. FROZEN SWEET PEAS

4. ONIONS

5. PAPAYAS

6. EGGPLANTS

7. ASPARAGUS

8. KIWIS

9. MANGOS

10. CABBAGES

11. CAULIFLOWER

12. CANTALOUPES

13. BROCCOLI

14. MUSHROOMS

15. HONEYDEW MELONS

PANTRY
STAPLES

SAVORY PANTRY ESSENTIALS

Here are the pantry staples you will need to make the recipes in this cookbook. I think we can all agree that cooking fats, vinegar, salt, pepper, etc. don't count as one of the five ingredients. It's really amazing what you can create with these pantry items, a few fresh things, and a store-bought Bobby Approved product. It's culinary magic!

Avocado Oil:

Goodbye, canola oil! Hello, avocado oil! The perfect neutral-flavored, high-heat oil that is heart healthy, unlike canola oil, which is derived from GMO grain, inflammatory, and horrible for your health.

Extra Virgin Olive Oil:

I'm not talking about a thirty-five-dollar bottle. Grab a bottle of California Olive Ranch EVOO. I mostly use it for drizzling over a dish, but once in a while to cook with too. Think of it as an everyday EVOO!

Virgin Coconut Oil:

Don't believe the hype; coconut oil is good for you! Yes, it's a saturated fat, but it's high in lauric acid and actually helps lower LDL cholesterol. Go for virgin coconut oil. That's the good stuff.

100% Grass-Fed Ghee:

O-M-Ghee, this liquid of the gods is not only tasty, it's also free of lactose and casein because it's pure milk fat—the milk solids have been removed.

Celtic Sea Salt®:

Are you ready to change your cooking game? This unrefined kosher sea salt is perfect for seasoning your food and the size of the crystals makes it easy to pinch. Typical salt is bleached, processed, and has anti-caking agents. Unrefined sea salt won't spike your blood pressure like iodized or bleached salt and has more flavor thanks to the natural minerals.

Himalayan Pink Salt:

This is a good second option for unrefined salt that is available everywhere.

Black Pepper:

Always buy black peppercorns and grind them fresh as needed. The pre-ground stuff is old and nasty!

Rice vinegar

Vinegar:

Rice vinegar, raw apple
cider vinegar with the
mother, and red wine vinegar.
Make sure the rice vinegar is
unseasoned, meaning it
has no added sugar.

**Raw Apple
Cider Vinegar**

**Red Wine
Vinegar**

Dessi is the baker in the family, and I wanted to make sure she shared a bunch of her sweet recipes in this book. For the most part, Dessi's recipes are paleo, and always gluten-free. Here are the pantry essentials you will need to stock up on to make her yummy dessert recipes.

100% GRASS-FED GHEE

Ghee is like butter, but even better! Make sure it's 100% grass-fed. I don't want any GMOs in your kitchen!

BUTTER

When it comes to butter, go for unsalted Kerrygold.

BAKING SODA

Nothing fancy here. Any type will do.

PURE VANILLA EXTRACT

No imitation vanilla. The real deal!

VIRGIN COCONUT OIL

Virgin coconut oil is a one-to-one replacement for any fat in sweet or savory recipes. Stick with unprocessed virgin oil.

SALT

Celtic Sea Salt® or Himalayan pink salt.

STORE-BOUGHT FLAVOR BOMBS

There's no way to make epic five-ingredient meals without a little help from store-bought products. There are some incredible products in this book made with best-in-class ingredients that deliver massive flavor. That's why I call them flavor bombs. They totally elevate a dish with no effort at all. I am talking about simmer sauces, curry pastes, enchilada sauces, BBQ sauces, condiments, and more. Traditionally speaking, these products are loaded with crap I would never want you to put in your body, but I have found products that have nothing but clean ingredients, and, best of all, they taste awesome! You will discover these bombs all throughout the cookbook and can buy them at most grocery stores.

Mirepoix: I cheated just a little bit for a few recipes in this cookbook! Any time you see mirepoix in a recipe list, it's a combination of red onion, carrots, and celery. But technically you can find precut mirepoix in the produce section of many grocery stores, including Trader Joe's. Some of the recipes were just impossible to make without the veggie base of a mirepoix, so hopefully you can forgive me! If you want to make the mirepoix instead of buying it, here's what you need:

Mirepoix:

- ½ a large red onion, finely diced
- 1 large carrot, peeled and diced
- 2 stalks celery, diced

If you like saving money, want to get most of the ingredients used in this cookbook, and don't feel like going to the grocery store, you should check out Thrive Market. They have been a trusted partner on the *FlavCity* YouTube channel for over four years. They have healthy and organic groceries with prices that are cheaper than the grocery store. I created a special landing page that has most all the ingredients used in this book along with an exclusive offer for *FlavCity* fans; go to thrivemarket. com/bobbyapproved. The membership fee pays for itself, and their 100% grass-fed ghee is one of my favorite things ever!

Crispy Crepes
Benedict • 45

BREAKFAST ALL DAY

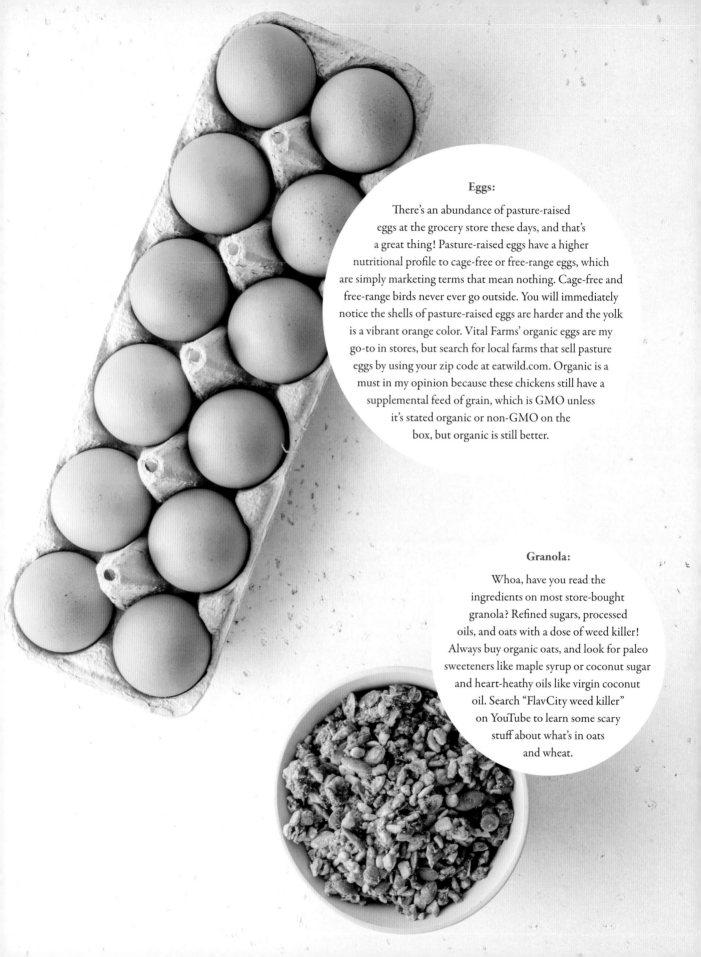

Eggs:

There's an abundance of pasture-raised eggs at the grocery store these days, and that's a great thing! Pasture-raised eggs have a higher nutritional profile to cage-free or free-range eggs, which are simply marketing terms that mean nothing. Cage-free and free-range birds never ever go outside. You will immediately notice the shells of pasture-raised eggs are harder and the yolk is a vibrant orange color. Vital Farms' organic eggs are my go-to in stores, but search for local farms that sell pasture eggs by using your zip code at eatwild.com. Organic is a must in my opinion because these chickens still have a supplemental feed of grain, which is GMO unless it's stated organic or non-GMO on the box, but organic is still better.

Granola:

Whoa, have you read the ingredients on most store-bought granola? Refined sugars, processed oils, and oats with a dose of weed killer! Always buy organic oats, and look for paleo sweeteners like maple syrup or coconut sugar and heart-heathy oils like virgin coconut oil. Search "FlavCity weed killer" on YouTube to learn some scary stuff about what's in oats and wheat.

Bacon:

Where is the love for the pig?!
You can find 100% grass-fed and
organic chicken at most grocery stores,
but when it comes to bacon and pork chops,
all they have is factory-farmed pork. Once
you try pasture-raised pork your life will be
forever changed. To find local farmers and
markets that sell pasture raised pork
go to eatwild.com and search
using your zip code.

Yogurt:

The yogurt aisle should be renamed
the dessert aisle. It's scary how much sugar
is in these tiny little containers. The whole
point of eating yogurt is to get some probiotic
bacteria in your gut. Well that doesn't mean much
when there's three to four teaspoons of added sugar also.
Sugar kills gut bacteria, which is why you only want
to eat plain, organic, or 100% grass-fed, whole-milk
yogurt. Whole milk is good for you, because that's
where the omega-3 fatty acids live. If you are
plant based, I've got you covered too. To
learn lots more search "FlavCity
yogurt" on YouTube.

MINI MEATBALL BREAKFAST HASH

- **8 ounces organic ground turkey**
- **1 red bell pepper, diced**
- **6 ounces baby spinach**
- **2 pasture-raised & organic eggs**
- **1 pound of frozen & thawed cauliflower rice**

You Tube To watch the video tutorial for this recipe, search "FlavCity keto hash" on YouTube.

 It's important that the **turkey** is organic. That means they have a non-GMO feed. **Peppers** and **spinach** are always on the dirty dozen, so I would also buy organic.

 Frozen cauliflower rice works best for this recipe as it's too hard to squeeze the water from freshly grated rice. Costco has an incredible deal on a five-pound frozen bag! No need to buy organic because cauliflower is on the clean fifteen list.

I like to do breakfast big on the weekends, and this hash is like a clean keto version of something you might find on a diner menu. Plus, who doesn't want to eat meatballs for breakfast?

Make the cauliflower hash by preheating a 10-inch nonstick pan just above medium heat with 2 tablespoons of avocado oil. Place the thawed cauliflower rice in a kitchen towel and squeeze as much water out as possible, then add the cauliflower to the pan along with ½ teaspoon of salt and a couple of cracks of pepper. Flatten the riced cauliflower with a spatula and allow to cook for 4 to 5 minutes until golden brown. Mix up the rice and flatten again, cook another 4 to 5 minutes. Keep doing this until the mixture is deep golden brown, remove from heat and keep warm.

Make the mini meatballs while the hash is cooking. Preheat a large nonstick pan over medium heat for 2 minutes with 2 teaspoons of avocado oil. Season the turkey with ½ teaspoon of salt and a few cracks of pepper and mix well. Form mini meatballs by dipping your hands in cold water and rolling them (this will prevent the mixture from sticking to your hands). Make sure they are small or they won't cook through. Add the meatballs to the pan and cook until crusty on all sides and cooked through—about 8 minutes. Remove meatballs and keep warm.

Raise the heat to medium-high, add a shot of oil to the same pan, and add the peppers. Cook until slightly charred, about 5 to 6 minutes, then add the spinach and cook until wilted, about 1 minute. Add ¼ teaspoon of salt and a few cracks of pepper, turn off the heat, and mix well.

To fry the eggs, add enough oil to coat the bottom of an 8-inch nonstick pan and preheat over medium-high. Once the oil is hot, add two eggs to the pan and season with a pinch of salt and a crack of pepper. Fry until the egg whites are golden on the bottom then tip the pan and spoon hot oil around the egg whites so they cook through. Carefully remove eggs from the pan.

Assemble the hash by putting the veggie mixture on top of the cauliflower hash, add the meatballs, and top it with the fried eggs. Enjoy!

There is a reason why **Celtic Sea Salt®** is in my pantry staples list for this cookbook, it's one of the best quality salts you can cook with. Not only does it taste great thanks to the natural mineral content, it's completely unrefined, which is not the case with that bleached white salt sitting in your pantry! Go for the Gourmet Kosher Celtic Sea Salt®, it will change your culinary life!

Macros per serving (makes 2):

CALORIES	NET CARBS	TOTAL CARBS	FAT	PROTEIN	FIBER
450cal	7g	15.6g	30.3g	28.6g	8.6g

PREP TIME: 1 MINUTE • COOKING TIME: 13 MINUTES • MAKES: 1 SERVING

VEGAN •

QUINOA BREAKFAST BOWL

- ¼ cup quinoa
- 1 tablespoon coconut cream
- Granola, for garnish
- Yogurt, for garnish
- Fresh fruit, for garnish

You Tube To watch the video tutorial for this recipe, search "FlavCity What I Eat in a Day" on YouTube.

This is my go-to breakfast Monday through Friday, and I never get tired of it! It's nutrient dense, loaded with texture, and this version is 100% dairy free.

To cook the quinoa, bring 2 cups of water to a boil. Before adding the quinoa, rinse it under water to remove any debris, then boil for 13 minutes. Drain very well and add to a serving bowl along with the coconut cream and mix well. Top with granola, yogurt, fruit, and enjoy!

When buying **coconut cream**, look for brands that don't add emulsifiers like guar gum. Although it's very common in nondairy milk, it's not needed in coconut milk. Too many gums can upset your stomach. My favorite brand is Let's Do Organic. They also make the best coconut milk, called Native Forest. Thrive Market and Trader Joe's make my second-favorite coconut milk and cream.

We eat grain-free and paleo **granola** at home, meaning no refined sugars or oats. My absolute favorite brand is Purely Elizabeth, followed by Autumn's Gold at Costco. They have a great price. Search "FlavCity granola" on YouTube to learn more about shopping for granola.

Yogurt can be a minefield! I highly suggest searching "FlavCity Yogurt" on YouTube to learn more. If you want the best-quality yogurt, 100% grass-fed and full fat is the way to go. Stonyfield 100% grass-fed and Greek style is one of the best, and my favorite plant-based yogurt is plain Greek-style Kite Hill and vanilla Lavva.

Macros per serving (makes 1):

CALORIES	NET CARBS	TOTAL CARBS	FAT	PROTEIN	FIBER
460cal	48.9g	55.9g	21.9g	11.7g	7.1g

KETO **TRUCKER'S BREAKFAST**

- 1 cup keto pancake mix
- 6 pasture-raised & organic eggs
- 2 tablespoons unsweetened and plain almond milk
- 10 strips of pasture-raised bacon, sugar-free

Trust me, HighKey makes the best tasting keto **pancake mix** you can find, and the ingredients are best in class. Even if you're not keto, these are the pancakes you want to put in your body since you won't feel bloated and like taking a nap after breakfast!

If you are on a low-carb keto diet and have been dreaming of eating a pancake breakfast, this one is for you! This pancake mix tastes epic and has the best ingredients on the market. Serve those flapjacks with crispy pasture-raised bacon and eggs and you will be one happy camper.

Preheat oven to 400°F for the bacon.

Make the pancake mix according to the instructions on the package. I like to use coconut oil instead of butter. It's very important to let the pancake batter sit for 10 minutes so the almond flour can hydrate.

To cook the bacon, line a sheet tray with a piece of parchment paper and top with bacon. I *never* cook on aluminum foil. I just don't think it's very safe. It's better to use unbleached parchment paper. Cook bacon for 13 to 16 minutes in the oven, remove, and keep warm. By cooking the bacon on a sheet tray, it will stay flat instead of curling up like when cooked in a pan.

Cook the pancakes according to the package instructions, but I like to add a little extra coconut oil to the pan so the pancakes get a nice color when cooking, and keep the heat just a turn below medium. When it's time to flip, be aggressive and do it with authority; these pancakes don't have any starch so they tend to be tough to flip. Finish cooking and keep warm in the oven with the bacon.

To fry the perfect sunny-side egg, use the same pan as the pancakes or an 8-inch one works even better. Preheat over medium-high heat and add the rendered bacon fat and enough avocado oil to cover the bottom of the pan. Once the oil is very hot, add the eggs and immediately pinch over some salt and cracked pepper. Make sure to use your splatter guard. Otherwise the oil will fly everywhere! Cook until the bottom of the eggs is deep golden brown. To help set the egg whites, carefully tilt the pan and spoon the hot oil over the whites. Remove from heat and serve with the pancakes and bacon, and enjoy!

Macros per serving (makes 2):

CALORIES	NET CARBS	TOTAL CARBS	FAT	PROTEIN	FIBER	SUGAR ALCOHOLS
817.5cal	3.2g	14.3g	72.7g	37.1g	7.1g	4g

Do yourself a favor and get some **pasture-raised bacon** by searching for local farms and markets near you at eatwild.com. Pasture-raised pork is unlike anything you have tried. If buying from the grocery store, look for organic bacon that has no sugar added.

 Pasture-raised eggs are the bee's knees, but even better are organic pasture raised. Organic means the chickens don't consume any GMO grains in their supplemental feed

CRISPY **CREPES BENEDICT**

- · **4 Crepini® Egg Wraps**
- · **4 whole pasture-raised organic eggs and 2 egg yolks at room temperature**
- · **1 tablespoon lemon juice**
- · **6 tablespoons grass-fed butter, melted**
- · **4 pieces prosciutto**

 To watch the video tutorial for this recipe, search "FlavCity eggs Benedict" on YouTube.

These keto egg wraps with cauliflower from **Crepini®** are awesome. We make sweet and savory crepes using them all the time, and the ingredients are top notch.

It had been years since I'd had runny poached eggs with fatty hollandaise sauce perched on top of a toasted English muffin. Reason being is because we don't eat gluten at home, but one day I decided to bake a cauliflower thin in a muffin tin and the idea for this recipe was born!

To make the crepe shells, preheat oven to 300°F and set the oven rack in the middle. Since the Crepini® crepes are so big at Costco, you will need to cut them a bit smaller to fit in a large muffin tin or try to find the smaller Crepini® at Walmart, Publix, or their website. Push the crepes about halfway down into the muffin tin and bake for 12 minutes or until they are slightly crispy and hold their shape. You can also use a low-carb tortilla for this recipe. Cut a smaller circle from it and spray with a touch of avocado oil before baking.

Make the hollandaise sauce by melting the butter over medium heat. Add the room temperature egg yolks to a blender along with the lemon juice and a pinch of salt. Blend on high for 15 seconds. With the machine running on medium, slowly add the warm melted butter, and once it's in, blend on high for 10 seconds. If the sauce is too thick, add 1 to 2 teaspoons of water and blend again.

To poach the eggs, fill a medium-size pot with 4 inches of water, bring to boil, and reduce to just below a simmer. There should be no bubbles or boiling in the water. Add 2 tablespoons of vinegar, swirl the water with a spoon, and then gently lower one egg at a time into the water. Cook eggs for 3 to 4 minutes or until the egg yolk is set to your liking and remove.

Assemble the keto eggs Benedict by putting one piece of prosciutto in the Crepini® cup, top it with a poached egg, and a drizzle of hollandaise sauce. Enjoy!

Macros per serving (makes 2):

CALORIES	NET CARBS	TOTAL CARBS	FAT	PROTEIN	FIBER
622cal	1.1g	1.1g	58.5g	24.1g	0g

PREP TIME: 1 MINUTE • COOKING TIME: 1 MINUTE • MAKES: 1 SERVING

POST-WORKOUT PROTEIN SMOOTHIE

- 10 ounces unsweetened & plain almond milk
- 1 scoop plant-based protein powder
- 3 tablespoons almond butter
- ½ frozen banana
- 1 tablespoon raw cacao powder

You Tube To see a video tutorial, search "FlavCity What I Eat in a Day" on YouTube.

 When buying **almond milk**, it doesn't have to be organic, but it should be free of sugar and the dreaded natural flavors. Always go for plain and unsweetened. This is true for any nondairy milk.

This is my go-to smoothie as soon as I get home from the gym. You won't find these ingredients at the juice bar; this is made from top-notch ingredients that your body needs after an epic workout.

Add everything to a blender and mix on high for 30 seconds. If the smoothie is too thick, add a splash of water.

My favorite **plant-based protein powder** is from Four Sigmatic. Not only are the ingredients clean, but it has seven (functional superfood) mushrooms and adaptogens—something I really believe in. Learn more about buying protein powder by searching "FlavCity protein powder" on YouTube.

Macros per serving (makes 1):

CALORIES	NET CARBS	TOTAL CARBS	FAT	PROTEIN	FIBER
532cal	25.8g	37.5g	32.5g	32.4g	11.8g

FLAVCITY SAVED MY LIFE! I AM IN MY TWENTIES, MORBIDLY OBESE, AND HAVE HAD HORRIBLE MEDICAL ISSUES! I'VE BEEN IN THE HOTPOT AND HAVE WEEKLY DOCTOR APPOINTMENTS. MY WHOLE BODY HURT AND WAS IN HORRIFIC PAIN. I AM ON SO MANY PILLS I CAN'T EVEN COUNT THEM. SICK ALL THE TIME AND DEPRESSED. MY MOM SENT ME ONE OF YOUR VIDEOS WHEN I DECIDED TO TRY AN ANTI-INFLAMMATORY DIET. WOW LIFE CHANGING! I'VE LOST WEIGHT, I'M HAPPY AND HEALTHY, AND MY CHRONIC ILLNESS... I HAVEN'T HAD A FLARE-UP OR EPISODE SINCE I JOINED THE FLAVCITY FAMILY. BOBBY, SERIOUSLY, THANK YOU FOR SAVING MY LIFE. I FEEL IN CONTROL OF MY LIFE AGAIN. I KNOW HOW TO SHOP AND WHAT TO BUY! OUR RUNNING JOKE IN THE FAMILY IS: "OK, BUT IS IT BOBBY APPROVED?" BOBBY, KEEP DOING WHAT YOU'RE DOING. LOVE AND LIGHT FROM LOS ANGELES AND THANK YOU!

–EMMA N.

NO-BAKE **GRANOLA**

- **3 cups of mixed nuts, roughly chopped**
- **2 teaspoons ground cinnamon**
- **1 tablespoon unsweetened cacao powder**
- **¼ cup maple syrup**
- **¼ cup of unsweetened shredded coconut flakes**

 To watch the video tutorial for this recipe, search "FlavCity granola" on YouTube.

 When buying **mixed nuts**, try to look for raw nuts that don't have processed oils like sunflower/safflower added and that are unsalted.

There are fantastic-quality store-bought granolas on the market, but if you want to make it at home, Dessi has you covered. This paleo granola only takes a few minutes and you don't even need to turn on the oven. Use it for my quinoa breakfast bowl or pour over a Bobby Approved nut milk for a healthy cereal bowl.

Preheat a large nonstick pan just below medium heat with 2 ½ tablespoons of coconut or avocado oil. Add the mixed nuts and cook for 5 minutes or until the nuts become lightly browned. Add ¼ teaspoon of salt and the cinnamon, cacao powder, and coconut flakes, and cook for another minute. Add the maple syrup and cook for 1 more minute. Take off the heat and check for seasoning. You may want a little more maple syrup. To make this recipe keto, replace the maple syrup with the same amount of sugar-free (Lakanto brand) maple syrup.

Allow to cool, break up any large chunks, and store in an airtight container on the counter for two weeks, if it lasts that long!

Cacao powder is raw and unprocessed while cocoa powder is processed. Both will work, but I prefer raw cacao for its health benefits. Get everything you need for my recipes at prices cheaper than the grocery store at thrivemarket.com/bobbyapproved, along with an exclusive offer for FlavCity fans.

Macros per serving (makes 8):

CALORIES	NET CARBS	TOTAL CARBS	FAT	PROTEIN	FIBER
409cal	14.2g	19.4g	35.7g	9g	5.2g

FLAVCITY HAS TAKEN ALL THE GUESSWORK AND
INTIMIDATION OUT OF GROCERY STORE SHOPPING.
DIFFERENT ITEMS ARE THOROUGHLY EXPLAINED WHY
THEY ARE BOBBY APPROVED OR NOT. THE VIDEOS AND
LIVESTREAMS ARE THE HIGHLIGHT OF MY DAYS. I HAVE
LEARNED AND RETAINED MORE INFORMATION FROM THIS
CHANNEL AND THIS COMMUNITY THEN I WOULD GET
FROM ANY OTHER SOURCE. I'M LOSING WEIGHT, GAINING
BACK CONFIDENCE, AND BECOMING THE HEALTHIEST
VERSION OF MYSELF. THANK YOU FOR EVERYTHING!

–SHAY S.

PREP TIME: **2 MINUTES** • COOKING TIME: **20 MINUTES** • MAKES: **2 SERVINGS**

BREAKFAST TACOS

- **6 pasture-raised and organic eggs**
- **4 slices pasture-raised bacon**
- **4–6 tortillas**
- **Salsa to serve**
- **1 avocado, for garnish**

You Tube To watch the video tutorial for this recipe, search "FlavCity breakfast tacos" on YouTube.

You Tube To watch a detailed grocery review on tortillas, search "FlavCity tortillas" on YouTube.

They don't sell breakfast tacos like this at any restaurant. It's only happening in your kitchen. We're talking best-in-class ingredients used to make some seriously tasty tacos.

Make the bacon by preheating the oven to 400°F and laying the bacon on a sheet tray lined with parchment paper. Bake in oven for about 15 minutes.

Make the scrambled eggs by vigorously whisking the eggs in a large bowl. The more air you beat in the fluffier the scrambled eggs will be. Heat a 10-inch nonstick pan over medium-low heat with 1 teaspoon of rendered bacon fat or ghee. Add the eggs and continuously stir with a rubber spatula. Keep cooking for 5 to 6 minutes until the eggs come together and are done to your liking. The goal is to keep stirring and break up the egg curds to keep them small. Season with a pinch of salt and pepper at the end, remove from heat, and cover with tin foil.

Prepare the other ingredients by warming the tortillas, heating the salsa in a small pot, and slicing the avocado.

Assemble the tacos with all of the toppings and enjoy!

My absolute favorite **salsa** is the double-roasted tomato salsa by Frontera. I just wish the tomatoes were organic, but ALDI makes an organic salsa from Casa Mamita that is really good too. Avoid any salsas with added sugar. It's just not needed.

The absolute best grain-free **tortillas** on the market are made by Siete. The cashew or almond flour tortillas have a very similar texture and flavor to flour tortillas. Pricey, but totally worth it! If you want corn tortillas, make sure they are non-GMO or organic. La Tortilla Factory makes an organic corn and wheat tortilla that has a great texture and flavor.

My go-to eggs at the store are Vital Farms' organic **pasture-raised eggs**. But I would recommend going to eatwild.com and searching for locally sourced pasture eggs by entering your zip code. They can be fresher and even higher quality!

Macros per serving (makes 2):

CALORIES	NET CARBS	TOTAL CARBS	FAT	PROTEIN	FIBER
625cal	23.1g	30.1g	47.5g	29.5g	7g

Crusty Lamb Chops with
Green Tahini • 66

CARNIVORE STYLE

TIKKA MASALA BEEF KEBABS

- 1 ½ pounds 100% grass-fed ground beef
- ½ cup plus 2 tablespoons tikka masala sauce
- 4 to 5 tablespoons roughly chopped fresh mint
- 1 ½ cups 100% grass-fed Greek yogurt
- 1 pack organic tri-color bell peppers

The best quality **yogurt** in my opinion is 100% grass-fed, organic, whole milk, and Greek style by Stonyfield. Greek-style yogurt is strained, which reduces the amount of natural sugar and gives it a lovely flavor. If you are dairy free, get the Kite Hill Greek-style plain almond yogurt. So good!

If you have never checked out the "simmer sauces" at the grocery store, you're missing out. The problem is that many of them are loaded with processed canola oil and added sugar. Luckily, I found a tikka sauce that has massive flavor and uses best-in-class ingredients. I absolutely love this recipe and I have a feeling you will too!

Make the beef kebab mixture by adding the ground beef to a large bowl along with ½ cup of the tikka sauce, 1 teaspoon of salt, a few cracks of black pepper, and 2 tablespoons of roughly chopped mint. Mix just enough to incorporate. If you overmix, the kebabs will be tough. Form the kebabs using metal or wooden skewers. You can find the ones I use on my Amazon Store (amazon.com/shop/flavcity). You will have enough mixture to make 4 kebabs. Chill them in the fridge for 30 minutes before cooking so they firm up.

Make the yogurt sauce by adding the yogurt to a small bowl and season with ¼ teaspoon salt, a couple of cracks of pepper, 1 tablespoon chopped mint, and mix well. Stir a couple of tablespoons of tikka sauce into the yogurt and check for seasoning. Adjust and set aside.

Cut the walls off the peppers and season with a shot of avocado oil and a little salt and pepper.

To cook the kebabs and peppers, preheat your grill to high for 10 to 15 minutes. Make sure to spray or brush the kebabs all over with avocado oil and carefully spray the grill grates. Grill the peppers until blistered on both sides for about 8 to 10 minutes total and cook the kebabs until the internal temperature is 155°F for about 10 minutes total. If the kebabs take on too much color, lower the grill to medium-low and close the door to create an oven effect.

Serve the kebabs with the peppers and tikka yogurt sauce. Enjoy!

I was blown away by the **tikka masala sauce** from Masala Mama! Not only is that a great name but the ingredients are next level, and when you only have five ingredients to work with, this product is a lifesaver.

Macros per serving (makes 3):

CALORIES	NET CARBS	TOTAL CARBS	FAT	PROTEIN	FIBER
685.7cal	13.8g	16.9g	43.3g	56g	3.1g

PREP TIME: **5 MINUTES** • COOKING TIME: **25 MINUTES** • MAKES: **2 SERVINGS**

KETO • PALEO •

CRISPY-SKIN LEMON CHICKEN

- 4 skin-on, boneless organic chicken thighs
- Juice of ½ lemon
- 1½ teaspoons capers
- 2 teaspoons fresh parsley, finely chopped
- 1½ pounds thick asparagus spears

- 1 cup beef bone broth

You Tube To watch the video tutorial for this recipe, search "FlavCity lemon chicken" on YouTube.

Asparagus is on the clean fifteen list. No need to buy organic, but look to buy thick spears, not thin pencil necks. They overcook so easily.

This is my favorite way to cook chicken—with the skin on and the bone removed. The skin gets crispy and adds extra fat so the meat won't dry out. Served with a zesty little pan sauce and tender asparagus, this is clean keto eating with serious crunch and flavor.

Buy some good quality organic bone-in chicken thighs and ask the butcher at the meat counter to remove the bone for you. They would be happy to do it, and make sure to save the bones in your freezer to make stock and bone broth.

To make the chicken thighs, first let them come to room temperature for 20 minutes and then season with a generous pinch of salt and pepper on both sides. Preheat a cast iron or nonstick pan over medium heat for 2 minutes with 1 tablespoon of avocado oil. Add the chicken skin side down and cook for 7 to 10 minutes or until the skin is deep golden brown. Flip and cook another 3 to 4 minutes until the chicken is cooked through. Remove the chicken from the pan, pour off all the fat, and cover the chicken loosely with foil. If the skin is not crispy, raise heat to medium-high and cook skin side down for another 4 minutes.

To make the sauce, drain excess fat and add 1 cup of water or bone broth to the pan along with the lemon juice, capers, and bring to a simmer. Cook for 10 minutes or until the liquid has reduced by half. Add 1 tablespoon of ghee to the pan along with the parsley, a pinch of salt, a couple cracks of pepper, and lower heat to low. Mix well, and cook another 1 to 2 minutes until the sauce has thickened up a bit. You may need 1 more tablespoon of ghee to thicken the sauce. Check for seasoning, turn the heat off the pan, and set aside.

To make the asparagus, bring a medium size pot of water to a boil and cut the tough bottom part off the asparagus. Add 1 tablespoon of salt to the boiling water along with the asparagus and cook for 2 to 3 minutes. Be on standby with a large bowl of cold water with ice. Bend the asparagus. If it's flexible but still has a snap left to it, immediately drain and add to the ice bath. Don't overcook it. That happens very quickly and easily. Allow to sit for 1 minute in the ice bath, then drain well.

Warm the asparagus in the pan with the sauce, plate it with the chicken, and pour over any leftover sauce and garnish with parsley. Enjoy!

If you follow me @flavcity, you know that I always have three bottles of this 100% **grass-fed ghee** in my pantry. The flavor is next level, and if you are sensitive to lactose or casein, ghee has none of that. It's pure milk fat. Grab a few bottles along with lots of other ingredients needed for my recipes at great prices over at thrivemarket.com/bobbyapproved. FlavCity fans also get an exclusive offer!

Macros per serving (makes 2):

CALORIES	NET CARBS	TOTAL CARBS	FAT	PROTEIN	FIBER
746.5cal	6.1g	13.2g	49.4g	64g	7.1g

BBQ BABY BACK RIBS

- 1 rack of pasture-raised baby back or spare ribs
- 1 tablespoon spice rub
- 2 teaspoons fine-ground coffee
- 4 ounces organic beer
- 1 ½ cups BBQ sauce

If you don't have a smoker or a secret spice rub, but still want some smokehouse-quality ribs, I've got you covered. Cooking these ribs low and slow in the oven sealed in a pouch with beer, store-bought spice rub, and ground coffee yields tender meat that falls off the bone with big-time flavor.

To make the spice rub, mix together 1 tablespoon of store-bought spice rub with 2 teaspoons of finely ground coffee. Season the ribs on both sides with the spice rub and let marinate in the fridge overnight. If short on time, you can skip the marinade and proceed with the recipe.

To make the ribs, preheat oven to 235°F and season the ribs with a generous pinch of salt on both sides. Tear 4 pieces of tin foil, big enough to fit the rack plus more, and wrap the ribs with the meaty side up. Seal the foil tightly except for one side and pour the beer along with 1 tablespoon of apple cider vinegar into the foil pack. Seal the last edge, place on a sheet tray meaty side up, and bake for 3 hours.

Once the ribs are done, remove from oven and kick on the broiler to medium. Brush BBQ sauce on both sides of the ribs and broil until bubbly and sticky on each side for about 3 minutes per side. Slice the ribs and enjoy!

Normally I would make my own **spice rub** for these ribs, but with only five ingredients that ain't gonna happen. I used the Costco brand organic no salt added spice rub and it was really good. They also sell pork barrel BBQ which has good ingredients, but since it has salt make sure to use less salt when seasoning the ribs. Look for rubs that have clean ingredients, no added sugar, MSG, corn meal, or preservatives. Easier said than done!

I highly recommend drinking **organic beer** like Michelob Ultra Pure Gold or gluten-free beer. Beer is made from wheat, and nonorganic wheat scores high in glyphosate.

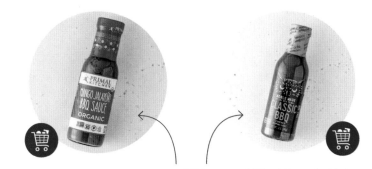

Have you read the ingredients on most **BBQ sauces**? Yikes! Tons of added sugar, caramel coloring, and more nasties. Look for Primal Kitchen BBQ sauce. Their Hawaiian or mango jalapeño BBQ sauce is so tasty with best-in-class ingredients. New Primal also makes a good paleo BBQ sauce.

Macros per serving (makes 2):

CALORIES	NET CARBS	TOTAL CARBS	FAT	PROTEIN	FIBER
1152.5cal	36.6g	36.6g	68g	80g	0g

DEALING WITH THE PAIN OF LUPUS AND RHEUMATOID ARTHRITIS IS EXHAUSTING. I WAS STUCK CONCERNING MY HEALTH UNTIL I CAME ACROSS FLAVCITY ON YOUTUBE. TO HAVE SOMEONE TO WALK ME THROUGH WHAT TO EAT, WHAT I SHOULD NOT EAT, AND WHY, HELPED ME TO UNDERSTAND MY DIAGNOSES. FOR YEARS I POISONED MY BODY WITH INFLAMMATORY OILS, SUGAR, AND PROCESSED FOODS. BOBBY'S INFORMATIVE, EDUCATIONAL VIDEOS TAUGHT ME WHERE TO BUY HEALTHY FOODS. MY LIFE HAS BEEN CHANGED AND EXTENDED. INSTEAD OF FEELING HOPELESS AND DEPRESSED, I ATTEND WATER AEROBICS THREE TO FOUR TIMES A WEEK, EAT HEALTHY, AND HAVE NO STRESSORS SHOPPING FOR BOBBY APPROVED FOODS. #FOREVERGRATEFUL

–ERIKA M.

PREP TIME: 5 MINUTES • COOKING TIME: 25 MINUTES • MAKES: 3 SERVINGS   KETO • PALEO •

CRUSTY **LAMB CHOPS WITH GREEN TAHINI**

- · **1 rack of lamb chops**
- · **½ cup tahini**
- · **2 cloves garlic**
- · **Zest and juice of 1 lemon**
- · **2 handfuls of fresh parsley**
- · **Smoked paprika**

 Rack of lamb should be your gateway into eating lamb for the first time, and Costco has the best deal on Australian lamb. The meat is so tender and perfect for a keto and paleo diet. The farming practices are top notch in Australia. When I visited a couple years ago, I was blown away by the endless rolling pastures of grassy goodness!

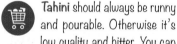 **Tahini** should always be runny and pourable. Otherwise it's low quality and bitter. You can use it for hummus, but the nutty flavor is fantastic is sauces and dressings too.

It boggles my mind that 40% of Americans have never tried lamb. You guys are missing out! Just look at the crust on those chops. That comes from a really hot cast iron pan and the flavor is righteous. Drizzle with green sauce and you are now a lamb believer.

Prepare the lamb chops. If you buy the lamb at a store that has a butcher, ask them politely to cut the rack into individual chops. This will save you time. If you buy them at Costco, you will have to do this yourself. Just use a sharp knife and pay attention to the bones at the base of the lamb. You will have to wiggle your way around it. Let the lamb sit at room temperature for 20 to 30 minutes. If you have smoked paprika, sprinkle some on both sides of the lamb at this time.

Make the tahini sauce by finely grating the garlic into the bottom of a liquid measuring cup. A 2-cup size is preferable. Zest the lemon and save that for later, and then add the juice to the garlic and let it sit for 5 minutes. This will take some of the raw flavor out of the garlic. Add ¼ teaspoon salt, a few cracks of pepper, a big handful of parsley, and the tahini. Have a cup of cold water ready and splash in ⅓ cup. Use a stick blender to mix everything and keep adding water until the consistency begins to loosen up. Blend until the parsley is well chopped and the consistency is somewhat loose. Check for seasoning. You may need more salt and/or lemon juice. If you don't have a stick blender, add everything but the parsley and whisk well in a bowl. Once the texture is achieved, add as much finely chopped parsley as needed. The stick blender is great for soups also. Get mine at amazon.com/shop/flavcity.

To cook the chops, preheat a large cast iron pan over medium-high heat for 3 minutes with 2 tablespoons of avocado oil. Season the lamb chops with a generous pinch of salt and a few cracks of pepper on both sides and add 4 to 5 chops to the pan. You don't want to overcrowd it. Cook for 2 to 3 minutes or until deep golden brown. Flip and only cook another 2 minutes. Repeat with remaining chops and keep the cooked ones warm.

To serve, spread some of the tahini sauce on a platter, place the chops down, spoon over more sauce, the reserved lemon zest, chopped parsley, and a drizzle of extra virgin olive oil. Enjoy!

Macros per serving (makes 3):

CALORIES	NET CARBS	TOTAL CARBS	FAT	PROTEIN	FIBER
773.3cal	6.4g	8.5g	59.3g	11.3g	2.1

BOBBY HAS CHANGED MY LIFE DRASTICALLY! HE'S

ALWAYS IN MY HEAD DURING GROCERY STORE HAULS

AND IF IT ISN'T CLEAN AND "BOBBY APPROVED," I PUT IT

BACK! NOURISHMENT TO THE BODY IS KEY TO FEELING

ENERGIZED AND HEALTHY AND BOBBY MAKES IT THAT

MUCH EASIER WITH ALL THE INFORMATION HE PROVIDES!

–KAESYN D.

GRILLED KOREAN SHORT RIBS

- 2 pounds grass-fed, flanken-cut short ribs
- ¼ cup plus 1 teaspoon gochujang
- ¼ cup maple syrup
- ½ cup creamy peanut butter
- 12-ounce bag of slaw mix

 It's very hard to find grass-fed, flanken-cut Korean short ribs. Go to shepherdmeats.com to find them. A FlavCity fan started this company and they have amazing-quality beef. FLAVCITY gets you 15% off.

 Look for **peanut butter** that only contains peanuts and salt. You will be shocked to see how many have palm oil and added sugar. Yuck! Search "FlavCity nut butter" on YouTube to watch a grocery review.

 Rice vinegar is a pantry staple, but make sure to buy one that has no added sugar.

The amount of flavor and texture achieved from just five ingredients is crazy in this recipe! If you're not familiar with gochujang, you will quickly discover the how tasty this umami bomb is and always have a container in your kitchen.

Make the marinade for the short ribs by combining the gochujang, 3 tablespoons maple syrup, 2 teaspoons rice vinegar, ½ teaspoon salt, and ½ cup of water in an 8 x 10-inch baking dish. Whisk well and add the short ribs, making sure the marinade is covering everything. Marinade the ribs for a minimum of 30 minutes, ideally 2 hours.

Make the slaw dressing by adding 1 teaspoon of gochujang to a blender with 2 teaspoons maple syrup, 2 ½ teaspoons rice vinegar, ½ cup peanut butter, ⅓ teaspoon salt, a few cracks of pepper, and ¼ cup of water. Blend on high. The mixture will most likely need another 3 tablespoons of water to make the consistency loose and pourable. Check for seasoning as you may need more of something based upon your preference. Set aside.

To cook the short ribs, preheat a grill to high for 10 to 15 minutes. Meanwhile, pour all of the marinade in a small pot, bring to a boil, and reduce to a simmer for 5 minutes or until reduced by half. Carefully spray the grill grates with avocado oil and pinch over some salt on the beef before placing on the grill. Season the other side with a bit more salt and cook until crusty on the first side for about 4 minutes and flip and cook another 2 to 3 minutes. Brush some of the reduced marinade over the ribs during the last 2 to 3 minutes. Remove from the heat and let rest under tin foil for a few minutes before you serve. If cooking in a pan, follow the same instructions and cook over medium-high heat.

Add the slaw mix to a large bowl and season with ¼ teaspoon of salt and a few cracks of pepper. Pour the peanut dressing over and mix well. Serve the short ribs with the slaw and enjoy!

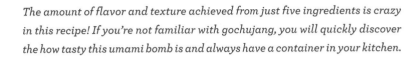 If you have never used **gochujang** before, it's time to change that! Most brands have GMO soybeans, added sugar, or gluten. Get the gochujang from Coconut Secret. The ingredients are next level, and honestly, anything they make is top notch!

Macros per serving (makes 3):

CALORIES	NET CARBS	TOTAL CARBS	FAT	PROTEIN	FIBER
1048cal	31.8g	40g	72g	68.2g	8.2g

PREP TIME: **5 MINUTES** • COOKING TIME: **15 MINUTES** • MAKES: **2 SERVINGS**

CHICKEN PESTO AND VEGGIES

- **2 organic boneless and skinless chicken breasts**
- **Two 8-ounce packs of precooked organic gluten-free grains**
- **7 ounces baby broccoli, halved**
- **5 ounces cherry tomatoes, halved**
- **¼ cup store-bought pesto sauce**

ALDI sells the best **organic precooked grain** packs called "90 second." There is a quinoa and brown rice pack with next level ingredients, but other stores sell varieties too. Just make sure to find one that uses organic grains and good oil, no canola or sunflower oil!

This recipe has two store-bought ingredients that will save major time in the kitchen. Also, if you always seem to overcook chicken breast, I've got you covered with a foolproof technique that is a game changer.

Prepare the chicken. The key to cooking crusty chicken breasts that are juicy AF is to pound them thinner. A big chicken breast will never cook evenly. To see exactly how to do this, search "FlavCity chicken breast" on YouTube. Place the chicken between two pieces of plastic wrap and firmly pound down and to the side with a meat mallet or rolling pin. You don't want a thin piece of chicken, just try to even out the lumps and bumps. Season the chicken breast with a healthy pinch of salt and pepper on each side and place aside.

To cook the veggies, preheat a large nonstick pan over medium-high heat with 2 tablespoons of ghee or avocado oil. Halve the baby broccoli so there is more surface area, then add to the pan and hold off on the seasoning. Cook for 5 minutes, stirring often, then add the halved tomatoes and cook until they burst and the broccoli is a bit charred. Season with ⅓ teaspoon of salt and a few cracks of pepper and remove from the pan.

To cook the chicken, preheat the same pan, or ideally a cast iron pan over medium-high heat for 3 minutes. Add 2 tablespoons of ghee to the pan along with the chicken. Push the chicken down so they make nice contact with the pan and let cook for 4 to 5 minutes or until a deep golden color has formed. Flip, turn the heat down to medium, and cook 3 minutes more. Remove from the heat and keep warm under tinfoil with the veggies.

Finally, **add the packs of organic grains** to the same pan over medium-high heat along with ¼ cup of pesto and ¼ cup of water. Mix well and add ¼ teaspoon salt and a few cracks of pepper. If the mixture is too thick, add more water as you want the consistency a bit loose. Check for seasoning and remove from heat.

Build a plate by putting some of the pesto grains on the bottom, scatter the tomatoes and broccoli, and top with sliced chicken and a good drizzle of extra virgin olive oil for the win! Massive flavor with only five ingredients, I love this recipe!

Most **store-bought pesto sauces** use highly processed oils. It really makes me mad! Only extra virgin olive should be used, so look for brands like Mezzetta, Gotham Greens, and DeLallo. If you can only find brands that use sunflower or canola, make sure it's non-GMO and expeller pressed, but only use these in a pinch.

Macros per serving (makes 2):

CALORIES	NET CARBS	TOTAL CARBS	FAT	PROTEIN	FIBER
1073.5cal	77g	90.6g	56.5g	52.7g	13.6g

PREP TIME: 2 MINUTES • COOKING TIME: 1 HOUR • MAKES: 4 SERVINGS

BEEF CHILI

- 2 pounds 100% grass-fed beef brisket or chuck
- Mirepoix (see page 28)
- 1 jar simmer sauce
- ½ cup organic red kidney beans
- Organic sour cream

 Organic dairy is a must. Otherwise the cows have a strict feed of GMO grains. Look for **organic sour cream** or cheese as a topping for this recipe.

When Dessi, Art, and I tasted this recipe we were blown away! How could I achieve such massive flavor with just five ingredients? Most chili recipes have way more! The answer is a store-bought simmer sauce that has next-level Tex-Mex ingredients and delivers massive flavor.

Soak the kidney beans overnight in water before starting this recipe.

Cut the beef into 1 ½-inch pieces, or better yet, ask the butcher at the store to do this for you! Preheat an electric pressure cooker to high or a stove-top cooker to medium-high with 2 tablespoons of avocado oil. Season the meat with a generous pinch of salt and pepper and sear half the meat until crusty on all sides for about 6 to 8 minutes. Repeat with the second batch, remove the beef, and immediately lower the heat to medium.

Add the mirepoix to the pot along with ¼ teaspoon of salt and a few cracks of pepper. Cook for 10 to 15 minutes or until the veggies are soft. Add the meat and juices back to the pot along with the jar of simmer sauce and 1 ½ cups of water. Drain the beans, add to the pot, mix well, and pressure cook on high for 45 minutes.

Once done, turn the heat off and allow the pot to rest for 10 minutes, then carefully release the pressure. You can also do this in a slow cooker on high for 6 hours or in a Dutch oven for 2 hours with the lid on cooking over a slow simmer.

Use a potato masher to break up some of the beef. This will help thicken the chili. Serve and top with a dollop of sour cream, and any other garnishes you have. Enjoy!

This recipe would not be possible without a **simmer sauce**, and I was blown away at the flavor and top-notch ingredients of Chosen Foods guajillo-pasilla simmer sauce!

Macros per serving (makes 4):

CALORIES	NET CARBS	TOTAL CARBS	FAT	PROTEIN	FIBER
822.3cal	24.1g	29.9g	56.8g	45.6g	5.8g

COMFORT FOOD

WILD MUSHROOM AND KALE TAGLIATELLE

- 8 ounces gluten-free egg tagliatelle
- 8 ounces wild mushrooms
- 5 cloves garlic
- 5 organic lacinato/Tuscan kale leaves
- 1 cup grated parmesan cheese

Wow, this **gluten-free tagliatelle** from Jovial is epic! It's made with organic brown rice flour and eggs and has the most silky texture ever. You want to avoid gluten-free pastas that use simple starches like corn, white rice, and tapioca. There is no need for those ingredients, and they are simple starches that spike your blood sugar even more! If using wheat pasta, I recommend buying organic. Search "FlavCity Weed killer" on YouTube to learn more.

*This is officially Dessi's favorite recipe in this chapter! You will be blown away at the power of good parmesan cheese and reserved pasta water. They make the creamiest sauce ever. Combine that with earthy wild mushrooms, kale, and one the best gluten-free pastas I've ever eaten. **Mangia!***

Bring a large pot of water to a boil for the pasta. Use more water than you think, about 1 gallon, because the pasta is quite starchy, and you will need the leftover pasta water for later.

While the water is heating, preheat a large nonstick pan just below medium-high heat with 1 tablespoon of ghee. Roughly chop the mushrooms into large bite-size pieces, not too small. Add mushrooms to the pan and cook for 8 to 10 minutes, stirring often until they are deep golden brown.

Meanwhile, mince the garlic and remove the stems from the kale and roughly chop. Add the garlic to the pan along with the kale, ⅓ teaspoon of salt, and a few cracks of pepper. Once the kale is wilted, turn the heat off the pan, about 3 minutes.

Add 1 tablespoon of salt to the boiling water and cook the pasta according to the box instructions. Normally I would add more salt, but there's so much cheese in this recipe it would get too salty. Save 1 cup of pasta cooking liquid and drain.

Place the pan with the mushrooms and kale over medium heat and add the pasta. This is go time. The goal is to add a handful of cheese to the pan along with a good splash of pasta water at the same time and stir vigorously. This will create the most beautiful silky cream sauce. Keep doing this until all the cheese is gone and add pasta water as needed. You will most likely need the entire cup of water. Taste the pasta since you may need to add more cheese.

Immediately serve the pasta and enjoy!

Macros per serving (makes 2):

CALORIES	NET CARBS	TOTAL CARBS	FAT	PROTEIN	FIBER
758.8cal	89.6g	95.3g	26.7g	36.1g	5.8g

Kale should always be bought organic because it's one of the dirtiest of the dirty dozen. Stick with lacinato kale. It's also called black, Tuscan, or dinosaur. It's much more tender and pleasant to eat than green curly kale!

Look for an 8-ounce assorted wild **mushroom** package in the produce section of the grocery store. They are a bit pricey, but so worth it. Whole Foods carries one that has gorgeous shrooms!

Parmesan:

Whatever you do, please don't use pre-grated parmesan cheese or that stuff in the green container. Look for Italian Parmigiano-Reggiano from Parma, Italy. This is the real deal! Luckily, it's available everywhere, and my favorite place to buy it is Costco. They have a 36-month-aged parmesan that is top notch.

Cheese:

When it comes to dairy, always go for organic or ideally 100% grass-fed. You can find organic cheese almost everywhere, and grass-fed is popping up in more and more grocery stores. If you can find grass-fed and raw, that would be ideal. Organic Valley has a 100% grass-fed and raw cheddar that is fantastic. Always grate cheese at home, never buy pre-grated. That stuff is inferior in every way and coated in wood pulp to prevent it from caking together. To learn more search "FlavCity Cheese" on YouTube.

FRIED **WILD RICE AND CHICKEN**

- ¾ **cup wild rice**
- **5 organic boneless and skinless chicken thighs**
- **½ cup plus 3 ½ tablespoons coconut aminos teriyaki sauce**
- **Mirepoix (see page 28)**
- **2 pasture-raised organic eggs**

Coconut aminos teriyaki sauce by Coconut Secret is always in my pantry! It's the most incredible go-to Asian sauce that is good for marinades or in a stir fry. The ingredients are epic, and the flavor is sweet and tangy!

We don't eat much rice at home, but when we do it's often wild rice, which is not actually rice. It's an aquatic grass, and because of that it has zero heavy metals and is more nutrient dense than brown rice. This fried rice has attitude and spunk thanks to the nutty and chewy texture of wild rice. You're going to love it.

Begin by cooking the wild rice in salted boiling water for 1 hour.

Marinate the chicken thighs in a zip-top bag with ½ cup of teriyaki aminos. Leave it on the counter for the entire time the rice is cooking.

Begin making the fried rice by preheating a large nonstick pan just above medium heat with 2 tablespoons of ghee or avocado oil. Add the mirepoix along with ¼ teaspoon of salt and a few cracks of pepper. Cook for 10 minutes or until the veggies have mostly softened. Whisk the eggs thoroughly and make a well in the center of pan, add eggs, cook until they come together, and then add the cooked and drained rice to the veggies and allow to cook for 3 minutes to evaporate any excess water in the rice. Add 3½ tablespoons of teriyaki and cook another 3 minutes. Check for seasoning since you may need a bit more salt or teriyaki. Take pan off the heat and set aside.

To cook the chicken, first remove it from the marinade, pat dry, and season with a good pinch of salt on each side. Using the same pan or a new one, preheat over medium-high heat with 2 tablespoons of ghee. Once the pan is hot, add the chicken and cook for 4 to 5 minutes on the first side, then flip and reduce heat to medium and allow to cook another 3 minutes. Remove from heat, spoon a dab of ghee over the top, and allow to rest for 2 minutes.

Serve the fried rice with sliced chicken on top and enjoy!

Macros per serving (makes 3):

CALORIES	NET CARBS	TOTAL CARBS	FAT	PROTEIN	FIBER
617cal	42.7g	46.6g	31.4g	39g	3.9g

MY GIRLFRIEND SUFFERS FROM CHRONIC INFLAMMATION
THAT DOCTORS COULDN'T SOURCE. AFTER WATCHING
FLAVCITY'S VIDEOS AND IMPLEMENTING HIS BUYING
STRATEGIES, SHE IS HAVING EXPONENTIALLY
FEWER INFLAMMATORY EPISODES. WE ARE
FOREVER GRATEFUL FOR YOUR ADVICE AND ARE
SHOWING ALL OF OUR FRIENDS YOUR VIDEOS!

–LOGAN J.

RISOTTO-ISH

- **Mirepoix** (see page 28)
- **10 ½-ounce box of risoni**
- **25 to 30 ounces of bone broth**
- **2 tablespoons fresh parsley, chopped**
- **Parmesan cheese**

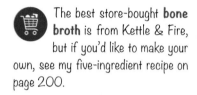

The best store-bought **bone broth** is from Kettle & Fire, but if you'd like to make your own, see my five-ingredient recipe on page 200.

This is my version of risotto! I replaced starchy, nutrient-dead white rice with one of the coolest things at Trader Joe's. Risoni is made from organic lentils and chickpeas, is loaded with protein and fiber, and tastes even better than rice! Just a few ingredients and my BFF bone broth make this risotto so darn tasty.

Preheat a 12-inch pan, preferably steel, over medium heat with 2 tablespoons of ghee. Add the mirepoix, ½ teaspoon of salt, a few cracks of pepper, and cook for 10 minutes or until the veggies are pretty soft. Meanwhile, warm the bone broth in a pot. Add the risoni to the pan along with another teaspoon of ghee and cook for 2 minutes. This will toast the risoni and add more flavor. Add enough bone broth to the pan to barely cover the risoni and mix well. Turn the heat just a notch below medium and cook for another 20 to 25 minutes, stirring often and adding more liquid when the pan gets dry. You don't need to stir nonstop, but you do have to give it lots of love.

If you run out of bone broth, use water, but make sure it's hot. After 20 minutes, check for seasoning. You will need more salt. You want the risoni to be al dente or have a little chew to it. Keep cooking until you get to that stage. Turn the heat off the pan when risoni is done, add 1 tablespoon of ghee, 1 tablespoon of chopped parsley, and a good grating of parmesan cheese.

Serve risoni with a generous grating of cheese on top, more parsley, and a drizzle of extra virgin olive oil. Enjoy!

I can't say enough great things about the **organic red lentil and chickpea pasta** risoni from Trader Joe's. I always say if you're going to eat carbs, make them count! If you can't get to Trader Joe's for the risoni, use Banza chickpea rice. It's not organic, which is a bummer, but works well. If using rice, use arborio rice.

Macros per serving (makes 2):

CALORIES	NET CARBS	TOTAL CARBS	FAT	PROTEIN	FIBER
681.5cal	78.6g	89.8g	11.5g	49.3g	11.3g

CHICKEN ENCHILADAS

- 1 ½ pounds organic boneless and skinless chicken thighs
- 1 ½ cup enchilada sauce
- Tortillas
- 1 cup organic cheddar or mozzarella, grated at home
- 3 to 4 radishes

Always grate **cheese** at home. The pre-grated stuff is inferior and coated in anti-caking powders like corn starch and wood pulp (cellulose).

I'm going to pat myself on the back for this one. Five ingredients, no corn, and massive flavors using some of the best store-bought items you can find.

To cook the chicken, add the chicken thighs, 1 cup of water, ½ cup enchilada sauce, 1 teaspoon salt, and a few cracks of pepper to a pressure cooker. Pressure cook on high for 12 minutes once pressure has been reached. When finished, let the cooker sit for 10 minutes off the heat then carefully release the steam. Let the chicken cool for 10 minutes, transfer to a cutting board, and shred it with two forks. Keep the chicken moist by adding some of the cooking liquid to it.

Meanwhile, slice the radishes very thin and place in a bowl. Cover with red wine vinegar and ¼ teaspoon salt. This will be your garnish later on.

To make the enchiladas, preheat oven to 400°F. Dip one of the tortillas in the warm chicken cooking liquid, add 3 tablespoons of pulled chicken, and carefully wrap. Smear some of the enchilada sauce on the bottom of an 8 x 10-inch baking dish and place the filled tortilla seam side down. Repeat with the remaining tortillas. Pour over a good amount of the enchilada sauce and then top with the grated cheese. Cover the baking dish tightly with tin foil and bake for 30 to 40 minutes until bubbly. Remove tin foil and broil for a couple minutes until the cheese is bubbly. Don't walk away!

Serve the enchiladas with pickled radishes and enjoy!

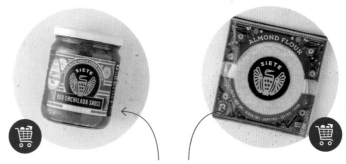

SIETE is one of the most Bobby Approved brands at the store, and everything they make is tasty and paleo. Their red and green **enchilada** sauce is next level, and the ingredients beat any other brand on the market. If you don't eat corn or wheat, go for their **almond flour tortillas**, the flavor and texture are on point!

EATING DECENTLY, BUT I WANTED TO DO EVEN BETTER

BECAUSE MY NEEDS HAVE CHANGED. I HAVE MADE MAJOR

CHANGES DUE TO LEARNING TO READ LABELS AND

ELIMINATING INFLAMMATORY OILS AND GRAINS FROM

MY DIET. THANKS, FLAVCITY! CONTINUE TO EDUCATE.

–DEBBIE J.

SPAGHETTI CARBONARA

- 3 slices organic or pasture-raised bacon
- 8 ounces gluten-free spaghetti
- ½ cup parmesan cheese, grated
- 4 pasture raised organic egg yolks
- ¼ cup fresh parsley, chopped

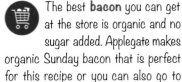

The best **bacon** you can get at the store is organic and no sugar added. Applegate makes organic Sunday bacon that is perfect for this recipe or you can also go to eatwild.com to find pasture-raised meat near you!

My go-to eggs at the store are Vital Farms' organic **pasture-raised eggs.** But I would recommend going to eatwild.com and searching for locally produced pasture eggs by entering your zip code. They can be fresher and even higher quality!

This is my take on a classic using best-in-class ingredients. It's really fun to watch the sauce come together with just pasta water, eggs, and cheese. Combine that with one of the best-quality and nutrient-dense pastas from the store, and you are good to go!

Chop the bacon into small pieces and place in a large nonstick pan. Set the pan over medium heat and cook until the bacon is crispy. Remove the bacon but leave all the fat in the pan.

Boil the pasta in heavily salted water according to the package instructions. If using the red lentil spaghetti like the one I used for this recipe, boil for 18 minutes to really soften it up.

Meanwhile, combine the egg yolks in a bowl with ¼ cup grated parmesan cheese, half the parsley, ¼ teaspoon salt, and a few cracks of pepper. Whisk well and set aside.

Once the pasta is ready, save 1 cup of cooking liquid then drain the pasta and put in the pan with the bacon fat. Turn the heat to medium-low and add the egg mixture to the pasta and mix very well, then immediately add ¼ cup of pasta water. Mix very well and then add half the remaining cheese and continue to mix very well. The goal is to create a creamy sauce using the yolks, pasta water, and cheese, without scrambling the eggs.

Add the rest of the cheese, a bit more parsley, a pinch of salt, a few cracks of pepper, and more pasta water as needed. Check for seasoning, as you may need more cheese or salt. Once the pasta is super creamy, turn the heat off and immediately serve it. Top with more cheese and some leftover parsley. Enjoy!

I used **organic red lentil spaghetti** from Whole Foods' 365 brand for this recipe, but some fans find it too al dente. You can also use Trader Joe's organic yellow lentil and brown rice pasta, which happens to be the best tasting and best textured gluten-free spaghetti on the market! Make sure your pasta is not made from starchy grains like corn or white rice. If using wheat pasta, I recommend buying organic. Search "FlavCity Weed killer" on YouTube to learn more.

Macros per serving (makes 2):

CALORIES	NET CARBS	TOTAL CARBS	FAT	PROTEIN	FIBER
692.5cal	62.5g	74.7g	21.9g	49.8g	12.2g

PREP TIME: 2 MINUTES • COOKING TIME: 15 MINUTES • MAKES: 2 SERVINGS

BEEF AND NOODLE STIR FRY

- 5 ounces sugar snap peas
- 4 green onions
- 8 ounces of 100% grass-fed steak, strip or flat iron
- ½ cup garlic coconut aminos
- 1 pound shirataki noodles

You all know how fond I am of keto **shirataki noodles**. My favorite brand is Pasta Zero by Nasoya. You can find it in the produce fridge section or refrigerated vegan section of Whole Foods and Walmart Supercenter. They have the best flavor and texture of any shirataki noodle I have tried.

This is a proper low-carb stir fry that will satisfy your noodle craving. Juicy marinated beef, blistered snap peas, and my absolute favorite, store-bought shirataki noodles.

Marinate the steak by cutting it into ¼-inch strips and placing in a bowl. Cover with ¼ cup of the garlic aminos and leave at room temperature.

You must cook the excess moisture out of the shirataki noodles. Otherwise they will water down any recipe you use them for. Preheat a large nonstick pan just above medium heat. Drain the noodles and give them a rinse under cold water. Shake off the excess water and cook in a dry pan for 7 to 8 minutes. Once the noodles stop releasing steam and the bottom of the pan is white, the noodles are ready. Remove and give them a rough chop. They tend to bunch together. Set aside.

Next, preheat a large nonstick pan over medium-high heat with 1 tablespoon of avocado oil. Once hot, add the snap peas and cook until the outside is well blistered for about 4 to 5 minutes. Finely slice the green onions and separate the white parts from the leafy green parts. Add the white part of the green onions to the pan along with the steak, making sure to shake off excess marinade. Season everything with ⅓ teaspoon of salt and a few cracks of pepper. Cook for 3 minutes, making sure the steak gets color on both sides. Add the shirataki noodles along with ¼ cup of garlic coconut aminos and cook for 3 minutes. Check the noodles for seasoning; you may need a pinch of salt or more aminos.

Turn the heat off, add the reserved green onions, and mix well. Serve and enjoy!

Garlic coconut aminos from Coconut Secret is the bomb! It's used as the marinade and stir fry sauce for this recipe, but you can also use their teriyaki sauce for this recipe.

Macros per serving (makes 2):

CALORIES	NET CARBS	TOTAL CARBS	FAT	PROTEIN	FIBER
420.5cal	19.6g	28g	21.3g	27g	8.4g

CAULIFLOWER MAC AND CHEESE

- ½ **large head of cauliflower**
- **1 heaping cup raw cashews**
- **¾ cup grated parmesan cheese**
- **Zest and juice of 1 lemon**
- **12 ounces pasta shells**
- **Cheddar cheese, freshly grated**

Cauliflower is on the clean fifteen list. No need to buy organic. Same is true for cashews.

I love these **pasta shells made from organic chickpeas**. Whole Foods' 365 brand makes a great one that I used for this recipe. You can also find shells from Banza, but they are not organic.

This cheese sauce is so darn tasty, you won't be able to tell it's made from veggies and nuts. A nutrient-dense version of mac that your kids will devour, guaranteed! In fact, this entire recipe would be vegan if I used nutritional yeast and vegan cheese, but daddy needs his Parmigiano-Reggiano.

Preheat oven to 400°F and bring a medium size pot of water to a boil. Cut the cauliflower into large bite-size florets and season the boiling water with 1 tablespoon of salt. Boil the cashews and cauliflower until the florets are soft, but not extremely mushy, about 8 to 10 minutes.

Save 1 cup of the cooking liquid, drain the cashews and cauliflower, and place them in a blender. Add ½ teaspoon of salt to the blender along with a few cracks of pepper, 2 teaspoons of extra virgin olive oil, ¼ cup grated parmesan cheese, zest of 1 lemon, juice of ½ a lemon, and ½ cup of the cooking liquid. Blend on high until very smooth. You will most likely need to add another ¼ cup of cooking liquid to loosen the sauce, maybe more. Check for seasoning as you may need more lemon juice or salt. Set aside.

Meanwhile, boil some water for the pasta shells and cook according to the box instructions. Save 1 cup of pasta water before draining.

In a large bowl, mix the pasta shells together with all of the cheese sauce and ¾ cup of reserved cooking water. Mix well and transfer to an 8 x 10-inch baking dish. If the mixture still looks dry, add another splash of water. Cover tightly with tin foil and bake for 30 minutes. Remove foil and top with ½ cup parmesan cheese, maybe more, and broil for a few minutes until the cheese is melted, but don't walk away! Instead of topping with parmesan, I would ideally use freshly grated cheddar cheese, but that would have been a sixth ingredient!

Allow to cool a couple of minutes, then enjoy!

Costco has a great deal on real Italian **Parmigiano-Reggiano**. The 36-month aged is my fave! Aged cheeses like parmesan have no lactose. It's eaten away by the bacteria during the aging process. So if you are lactose intolerant, you have nothing to worry about!

Macros per serving (makes 3):

CALORIES	NET CARBS	TOTAL CARBS	FAT	PROTEIN	FIBER
867cal	75.5g	96.3g	35g	43.8g	20.8g

I WAS ON THE VERGE OF DIABETES, WITHOUT A
CARE IN THE WORLD ABOUT WHAT I PUT IN MY
BODY, AND ALWAYS FELT SICK AS A CONSEQUENCE.
NOW I CARE ABOUT THE INGREDIENTS IN MY FOOD
AND I HAVEN'T FELT THIS GOOD IN YEARS!

–TONY Y.

PREP TIME: **5 MINUTES** • COOKING TIME: **35 MINUTES** • MAKES: **3 SERVINGS**

KETO •

KETO CAULIFLOWER MASH

- 1 head cauliflower
- 3 cloves garlic
- 1 cup organic heavy cream
- 5 fresh sage leaves
- 1 cup organic or grass-fed white cheddar cheese

If you are on a low-carb keto diet this is the closest you can get to actual mashed potatoes. The key is roasting the cauliflower; that adds such a nutty flavor. Also key is cream and butter, lots of it!

Preheat oven to 450°F and cut the cauliflower into bite-size florets. Toss the florets with 2 tablespoons of avocado oil, 1 teaspoon salt, and a few cracks of pepper. Arrange on a sheet tray along with 3 cloves of garlic in their paper skin and bake in the oven. Remove garlic after 10 minutes and cook cauliflower for 30 to 35 minutes total or until the edges of the cauliflower get toasty.

Meanwhile, add the cream to a small pot along with the sage, ¼ teaspoon salt, and a few cracks of pepper. Warm the cream over low heat so the flavors can infuse for about 10 minutes, but make sure not to boil. Make sure it's warm when you add it to the blender.

Transfer roasted cauliflower to a blender along with the cheese and half of the warm cream. Don't add the sage. Blend on high and keep adding more warm cream until you get the texture you want. You will likely need all of the cream. Check for seasoning as it may need more salt. Serve and enjoy!

Cauliflower is on the clean fifteen list, no need to buy organic.

Kerrygold Dubliner (Costco has amazing price) or Organic Valley **white cheddar** works great for this recipe.

When it comes to dairy, always go organic, or better yet, grass-fed. I wish someone would make a 100% grass-fed **cream** already!?

Macros per serving (makes 3):

CALORIES	NET CARBS	TOTAL CARBS	FAT	PROTEIN	FIBER
494.3cal	11.4g	18.6g	42.6g	14.9g	7.1g

HONEY **GLAZED CARROTS**

- 1 teaspoon fresh thyme leaves
- 6 cloves of garlic
- 1 pound rainbow carrots, with stems on
- ½ cup freshly squeezed orange juice
- 3 tablespoons local USA honey

Look for **rainbow bunch carrots** at Whole Foods. The colors are brilliant, and your kids will be more likely to scarf them down.

This could be one of my favorite side dishes! The carrots are so sexy, sweet, and blistered that your picky eaters are guaranteed to like them and maybe ask for seconds.

Add 2 tablespoons of ghee to a large cast iron or nonstick pan along with the thyme leaves. To strip the thyme leaves, just run your fingers in the opposite direction from how they grow. You could also be lazy and just toss 10 sprigs in the pan and the leaves will eventually fall off. Gently smash the garlic cloves, remove the paper, and add them to the pan set over medium heat. Cook until the thyme crackles and the garlic has a little golden color, about 4 minutes.

Wash the carrots and remove the green stems. Slicing from top to bottom, quarter the carrots. Some pieces may be too long so you can halve as needed. Add the carrots to the pan and cook for 5 minutes or until the carrots begin to take on some color. Add the orange juice and honey, stir well, and cover the pan with a lid or just use a sheet tray to cover it. Cook for 10 to 12 minutes, stirring a few times, then remove the lid and cook until the liquid begins to reduce and become bubbly like caramel.

At this point poke the carrots with a knife. If they feel too raw, add another ¼ cup of orange juice and put the lid back on for 5 minutes. Season with ½ teaspoon salt, a few cracks of pepper, and only turn the heat off once the sauce gets really sticky and it's on the edge of burning. It's a fine line!

Serve and enjoy!

It's really important to buy **local raw honey** produced in the USA. Imported honey could be cut with brown rice syrup. Raw honey is not heated so all the good living nutrients are still alive. Of course you kill them in this recipe, but you get the point!

Macros per serving (makes 2):

CALORIES	NET CARBS	TOTAL CARBS	FAT	PROTEIN	FIBER
349cal	49.7g	56.6g	14.6g	2.5g	6.9g

Lemon Olive Oil Cake • 123

When it comes to baking, I turn it over to my wife Dessi! She has loads of easy dessert recipes that are made with top-notch ingredients, all of them are gluten free, and most of them are paleo!

DESSI'S PALEO SWEETS

PALEO BAKING ESSENTIALS

Coconut Sugar:

If you have never tried coconut
sugar, be prepared for tasty goodness.
It's made from the nectar of the coconut
blossom, has a nutty caramel flavor, and
is lower on the glycemic index than cane
sugar. It's a one-to-one replacement
for sugar, and even goes great
in a cup of coffee!

Maple Syrup:

Dessi loves to bake with
maple syrup, so stock up! It
has such a lovely flavor, is low on
the glycemic index, and can also
be used for savory recipes like
my shrimp cakes in the
seafood chapter.

Cacao Powder:

Is that a spelling error? Nope,
cacao is raw chocolate beans that have
not been processed or heated. Cocoa
has been processed. That's not a bad thing,
but Dessi prefers the flavor and the health
benefits of raw cacao. You can use either
one. Just make sure it's unsweetened
and has no other ingredients
expect cacao/cocoa.

Bob's Red Mill Paleo Baking Flour Mix:

This is one of the best quality gluten-free and paleo baking mixes on the market. Instead of being loaded with cheap starches and fillers, it has almond flour, coconut flour, and just the right amount of binders like arrowroot and tapioca starch. It is a bit pricey, but I would get the two-pound bag for a good price over at thrivemarket.com/bobbyapproved, or you can make your own version of this flour mix at home! Here's the recipe:

Almond Flour:

Almond farmers rejoice, almonds have taken over! This keto and paleo flour is great for both sweet and savory recipes. Don't be confused: almond flour is not the same as almond meal. Meal has the skins still on; flour is blanched and ground very fine.

Paleo Flour Mix (makes 4 cups):

- 2 cups almond flour
- 1 cup arrowroot starch
- ⅔ cup coconut flour
- ⅓ cup tapioca starch

Arrowroot Starch:

Gluten-free and paleo desserts need to have a binder to bring everything together. Dessi loves arrowroot starch, but you can also use tapioca starch if that's what you have. One thing you will notice about store-bought gluten-free items is that they are mostly made of starches and fillers, which is not good because they offer no nutrition, just pure carbs. Dessi's desserts are never like that. They are balanced and well proportioned. To learn more about the best gluten-free products at the store search "FlavCity gluten-free" on YouTube.

BULGARIAN **HONEY COOKIES**

- 1 pasture-raised and organic egg
- ¼ cup of local honey
- 2 cups blanched almond flour
- 1¼ teaspoon cinnamon
- ¾ cup paleo or sugar-free chocolate chips

PANTRY

- 3 tablespoons virgin coconut oil, melted
- 1 teaspoon vanilla extract
- 1 teaspoon baking soda

You can't beat the price of **almond flour** at Costco or Sam's Club. Just keep in mind that almond meal is completely different than almond flour. Stick with flour.

Dessi grew up eating medenki in Bulgaria—soft honey cookies half dipped in chocolate. She wanted to share the recipe with you guys, but without the gluten and refined sugar. The texture of these honey cookies is fantastic, soft and chewy, and they go great with a cup of coffee or tea.

Preheat oven to 350°F. Whisk the egg in a bowl and add the melted coconut oil, vanilla extract, and honey.

Place the almond flour, baking soda, and ¼ teaspoon of salt in a small food processor and pulse a couple of times to mix the dry ingredients. Pour the wet ingredients on top of the dry and process until the dough becomes smooth, about 30 seconds. If you don't have a food processor, use a hand mixer or do it by hand. Just make sure to mix all ingredients very well.

Place some coconut oil on your hands and using a cookie dough portion scooper (that is about 1.2 tablespoons in size) or a spoon, scoop some dough and form it into a ball. Place the ball on a sheet tray lined with parchment paper and gently press down on top to flatten it into about a 1 ½-inch circle. Continue with the rest of the dough. You should end up with about 19 cookies.

Bake in a 350°F oven for about 12 to 14 minutes. The cookies will still be soft to the touch when you pull them out. Let them cool down and then melt the chocolate or chocolate chips over a double boiler. Decorate the cookies with the melted chocolate and let the chocolate cool so it can harden.

Cookies will last on the counter for a day or 3 days in the fridge.

Make sure to buy **locally sourced honey**. It's scary what happens with imported honey from certain parts of the world. Watch **Rotten** on Netflix, the honey episode.

Macros per serving (makes 19):

CALORIES	NET CARBS	TOTAL CARBS	FAT	PROTEIN	FIBER
133cal	6.5g	8.4g	10.5g	3.2g	1.9g

My favorite **chocolate chips** are the Gems from Hu Kitchen. They are the cleanest chips I have ever seen and are made with top-quality chocolate and coconut sugar. You can also use the semi-sweet chocolate chips from Lily's. They are sweetened with stevia and are low carb. The net carbs per serving drop to 4.7g if using sugar-free chips.

STICKY DATE PUDDING

- 2 cups paleo flour mix (see page 107)
- 1 ¼ cup medjool dates, pitted and chopped (about 6 ½ oz or 10 dates)
- 3 pasture-raised and organic eggs
- 1 cup coconut sugar
- 1 can (13 ½ oz) full-fat coconut milk

PANTRY

- 3 teaspoons vanilla extract
- ½ cup grass-fed ghee
- 1 teaspoon baking soda

Coconut sugar is also called coconut palm sugar. It's an incredible paleo sweetener that has a nutty, caramel flavor. Grab the sugar and everything else you need for these recipes on my special landing page at thrivemarket. com/bobbyapproved, along with an exclusive offer for FlavCity fans.

If you're looking for a decadent dessert that tastes sinful but uses really clean ingredients, this one is for you! Dense and sweet cake drenched in nutty vegan caramel sauce.

Preheat oven to 325°F. Add 2 cups of paleo baking mix to a large bowl along with ¼ teaspoon salt and ½ teaspoon baking soda. Mix well and set aside.

Place chopped dates in a pot with 1 cup of water over medium heat until the mixture starts to boil, turn heat down to a simmer, and cook for 5 minutes until the mixture gets very soft and jammy. Remove from heat and add ½ teaspoon of baking soda to the date mixture and beat with hand mixer until very smooth.

In a separate bowl, use a hand mixer to beat 3 eggs, ½ cup coconut sugar, and 2 teaspoons of vanilla on high for about 5 minutes and add ½ cup ghee and beat for another 30 seconds. Add the flour mixture to the egg mixture and beat for 1 minute until everything is fully incorporated. Fold in the date mixture and stir until just combined.

Smear a little bit of ghee inside of a mini Bundt cake or muffin tin, sprinkle over a bit of paleo flour mix, and fill the tins almost to the top with batter.

Bake for 30 to 33 minutes or until a toothpick comes out clean, and allow to cool.

To make the caramel sauce, add the coconut milk to a small pot along with ½ cup coconut sugar, ½ teaspoon salt, and bring to boil. Immediately turn the heat down to a gentle simmer for 40 to 50 minutes while stirring occasionally with a wooden spoon. The sauce will reduce and turn a deep caramel color. The sauce will thicken once it cools down, so don't worry if it looks a bit loose. Remove from the heat and stir in 1 teaspoon of vanilla extract, set aside to cool.

Let the puddings rest in the tin for about 15 minutes and then pop them out. Drizzle caramel sauce all over just before serving. Enjoy!

 Look for **medjool dates** with the pits. They are big, fat, and much juicer than pitted ones.

Macros per serving (makes 6):

CALORIES	NET CARBS	TOTAL CARBS	FAT	PROTEIN	FIBER
672cal	68.4g	74.5g	38.2g	9.9g	6.1g

Look for **full-fat coconut milk**. The reduced fat version has more water. Who wants that? Also, stick with brands that don't use gums or emulsifiers, like Native Forest (my fave) or Thrive Market.

The **paleo flour mix** from Bob's Red Mill is fantastic. The price on Thrive Market is great, but if you want to save some cash, you can make your own. See recipe on page 107.

I HAVE AN INFLAMMATORY AUTOIMMUNE DISEASE. I'VE

BEEN DOING KETO FOR INFLAMMATION REDUCTION

AND WITH HELP FROM YOUR RECIPES AND SHOPPING

VIDEOS I HAVE LEARNED HOW TO MAKE DELICIOUS,

HEALTHY RECIPES FOR MYSELF AND MY FAMILY. THE

INFLAMMATION IN MY BODY HAS DECREASED SIGNIFICANTLY

IN THE LAST FEW MONTHS. THANK YOU, FLAVCITY!

—ANNETTE D.

PALEO •

5 Ingredient Semi-Homemade Meals |

BERRY PANNA COTTA

- **1 ¼ cup fresh or frozen organic berries (blueberries, strawberries, raspberries)**
- **1 cup coconut cream**
- **3 tablespoons maple syrup**
- **1 ¼ teaspoon gelatin**
- **½ teaspoon lemon juice**

The texture, color, and flavor of this panna cotta is perfection. The fact that it's dairy free is crazy, plus the coconut cream is loaded with healthy MCTs.

Place the berries in a small pot, bring to boil, and simmer on very low heat for about 15 to 20 minutes.

In the meantime, sprinkle the gelatin over 1 ¼ tablespoon of water and let the gelatin expand and soften.

Place the coconut cream, hot berries, and maple syrup in a blender and blend on high for about 10 seconds until very smooth. Strain through a fine sieve and then pour the mixture back into the pot and heat up. Add the softened gelatin and stir until fully incorporated. Turn off the heat and stir in ½ teaspoon of lemon juice.

Pour into small ramekins and let cool. Then transfer to the refrigerator. Let the panna cotta set in the refrigerator for at least 1 to 2 hours.

Garnish with fresh berries and lemon zest before serving.

Berries are always on the dirty dozen list, so try to buy organic.

Always buy real **maple syrup**, not the ones made with cane sugar and artificial flavors. It's one of the best paleo sweeteners and is lower on the glycemic index. I like to scoop the big jug at Costco.

Coconut cream is always in my pantry, but try to avoid ones with gums and emulsifiers because they are not needed and make the texture a bit slimy. Go for the Let's Do Organic or Thrive Market brand.

Macros per serving (makes 4):

CALORIES	NET CARBS	TOTAL CARBS	FAT	PROTEIN	FIBER
359.8cal	18.8g	19.9g	29.4g	0.3g	1.1g

CHOCOLATE CHIP COOKIES

- 1 ¼ cup paleo flour mix (see page 107)
- ½ cup plus and 3 tablespoons coconut sugar
- ⅓ cup creamy almond butter
- 1 pasture-raised and organic egg
- ¾ cup paleo or sugar-free chocolate chips

PANTRY

- 1 stick (½ cup) unsalted grass-fed butter (or ghee, coconut oil), room temperature
- 1 teaspoon baking soda
- 1 teaspoon vanilla extract

These cookies remind me of the ones I used to eat as a kid. I can't say the brand name, but it rhymes with bent-a-mins! The only difference is Dessi makes these with best-in-class ingredients and I highly recommend eating two while watching Netflix!

Preheat oven to 350°F and line a sheet tray with parchment paper. Into a medium bowl, add the paleo mix, baking soda, and ¼ teaspoon of salt. Mix well and set aside. In another bowl, beat the sugar and butter (or coconut oil/ghee) together for 1 minute on high using a hand mixer. Add the almond butter, vanilla, and beat on medium for another 15 seconds to combine. Add the egg and beat to combine once again.

Add the dry mix to the wet mix and stir with a spatula until thoroughly combined. Add the chocolate chips and mix well. Cover the batter with plastic wrap and chill the batter for at least 30 minutes in the refrigerator or even overnight.

Use a cookie scoop or spoon and place dough a few inches apart on sheet tray. You will have more dough than can fit on one sheet tray. Bake for 13 minutes or until lightly golden around the edges. Let cool on the sheet tray and enjoy!

I know a bunch of you are thinking: "Can I make these keto by using monk fruit and almond flour?"—the answer is no. The cookies will fall apart. Stick with the **paleo mix** from Bob's Red Mill or make the mix at home using the recipe on page 107.

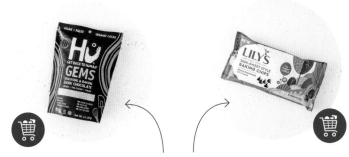

As I said before, my favorite **chocolate chips** are the Gems from Hu. They are the cleanest chips I have ever seen and made with top quality chocolate and coconut sugar. You can also use the semi-sweet chocolate chips from Lily's. They are sweetened with stevia and are low carb. The net carbs per serving drop to 10.8g if using sugar-free chips.

→

Macros per serving (makes 18):

CALORIES	NET CARBS	TOTAL CARBS	FAT	PROTEIN	FIBER
179.5cal	13.7g	15.4g	12.3g	3g	1.8g

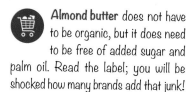 **Almond butter** does not have to be organic, but it does need to be free of added sugar and palm oil. Read the label; you will be shocked how many brands add that junk!

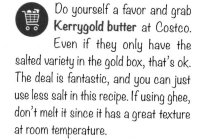 Do yourself a favor and grab **Kerrygold butter** at Costco. Even if they only have the salted variety in the gold box, that's ok. The deal is fantastic, and you can just use less salt in this recipe. If using ghee, don't melt it since it has a great texture at room temperature.

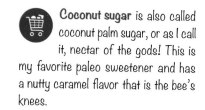 **Coconut sugar** is also called coconut palm sugar, or as I call it, nectar of the gods! This is my favorite paleo sweetener and has a nutty caramel flavor that is the bee's knees.

HONESTLY, I THOUGHT I WAS EATING "HEALTHY" UNTIL I

CAME ACROSS YOUR VIDEOS OVER A YEAR AGO. READING

LABELS ALONE BLEW MY MIND. I HAD NEVER READ AN

INGREDIENT LIST OR LABEL BEFORE THEN. NOW, I HAVE

ALL THE TOOLS AND INFORMATION TO SHARE WITH MY

FRIENDS AND FAMILY! I REALLY HOPE YOU KNOW HOW

MANY LIVES YOU HAVE CHANGED. I CAN'T EVEN TELL YOU

HOW MANY TIMES I'VE EVEN OFFERED INFORMATION

AND SHARED YOUR PAGE WITH TOTAL STRANGERS, LOL!

—CAMAY C.

LEMON OLIVE OIL CAKE

- **2 cups paleo baking mix (see page 107)**
- **4 pasture-raised and organic eggs**
- **½ cup plus 2 tablespoons maple syrup**
- **2 lemons**
- **½ cup sliced almonds**

PANTRY

- **½ teaspoon baking soda**
- **½ cup extra virgin olive oil**
- **1 teaspoon vanilla extract**

In my mind, I'm eating this cake on the Amalfi Coast while sipping on an espresso. This cake is such a joy to eat, the lemon zings your palate, and it is light as a feather. You won't miss the gluten or dairy!

Preheat oven to 325°F and cut a piece of parchment paper to fit in the bottom of a 9-inch springform pan. In a large bowl, mix the paleo baking mix, baking soda, zest of 2 lemons, and ¼ teaspoon salt. Separate the egg yolks and egg whites in two medium-size bowls. Use a hand mixer to beat the egg yolks with ½ cup maple syrup until fluffy. Add the olive oil, ¼ cup of lemon juice, vanilla extract, and beat to combine.

Beat the egg whites in another bowl until stiff consistency. Add the dry mixture to the wet egg yolk mixture and mix well. Gently fold in the egg whites with a spatula (don't stir). Make sure the egg whites are fully incorporated. Pour the batter into the prepared springform pan, top with sliced almonds, and bake for 45 to 50 minutes or until a toothpick comes out clean.

While the cake is baking, **make the glaze** by adding 2 tablespoons of lemon juice to a small pot along with 2 tablespoons maple syrup and 2 tablespoons of water. Bring to a boil over medium-high heat and immediately turn off the heat.

Once the cake has come out of the oven and cooled, warm up the glaze and brush it over the cake. Hot glaze on cool cake gets absorbed best. Serve and enjoy!

Bob's Red Mill **paleo mix** is the bomb! Yes, it's a bit pricey, but you can make your own paleo baking mix, see recipe on page 107.

Make sure to buy real deal **maple syrup**, not the cheap ones made with sugar and caramel coloring. I usually buy the big jug at Costco. It's organic, but that's not necessary for maple syrup.

My favorite eggs at the store are from Vital Farms. I would get the **pasture-raised and organic eggs** in the orange box.

Macros per serving (makes 8):

CALORIES	NET CARBS	TOTAL CARBS	FAT	PROTEIN	FIBER
379.3cal	28.1g	32.1g	24.3g	8.5g	4g

I'M SO GRATEFUL FOR FINDING FLAVCITY. MY
PERSPECTIVE ON HEALTHY COOKING HAS COMPLETELY
CHANGED SINCE LEARNING WHAT FOODS ARE TRULY
GOOD FOR ME AND WHICH ONES TO AVOID. I FEEL
BETTER THAN EVER KNOWING EXACTLY WHAT TO
PUT INTO MY BODY FOR THE MOST NUTRITION!

–ROBBIE B.

PALEO •

5 Ingredient Semi-Homemade Meals |

VANILLA CUSTARD WITH STRAWBERRY JAM

- 13 ½-ounce can full-fat coconut milk
- 5 pasture-raised and organic egg yolks
- ⅓ cup maple syrup
- 2 tablespoons arrowroot starch
- 1 ½ cups fresh or frozen strawberries, sliced

PANTRY

- 1 teaspoon vanilla extract
- ½ tablespoon virgin coconut oil

Look for full-fat **coconut milk**. The reduced-fat version has more water. Who wants that!? Native Forest makes the best quality and best tasting coconut milk on the market. There are no added gums, yet the texture is so darn smooth and creamy!

These are the types of sweets you want to give your kids or even the big kids, there's nothing to feel guilty about when using ingredients like these. The custard is soft and creamy, and the berries add just enough tang.

Add the coconut milk to a medium-size pot set over medium-low heat, whisking occasionally until hot but not boiling. Meanwhile, add the egg yolks, maple syrup, and arrowroot starch in a bowl. Whisk well until mixture is smooth. Set aside.

Remove the coconut milk from the heat, and while whisking, very slowly start pouring the coconut milk into the egg mixture, whisking vigorously. You don't want to scramble the eggs. I recommend using a small ladle or a measuring cup to pour the milk slowly until all the milk is whisked into the egg mixture. Then pour the mixture back into the saucepan.

Heat the custard over medium heat, whisking almost constantly until it starts to get thick like pudding and bubble for about 5 to 7 minutes. Remove from the heat and whisk in the vanilla extract and the coconut oil.

Cool to room temperature, and if you'd like to store it in the fridge, place a piece of plastic wrap directly on top of the custard.

Cook the sliced strawberries in a small pot over medium heat until they soften and get jammy for about 10 to 15 minutes. Add ½ tablespoon of maple syrup, stir well, and remove from heat. You can store the strawberry jam in the fridge until ready to build custard cups.

Build the custard and strawberry cups and enjoy!

Strawberries are always on the dirty dozen list, so I would always buy organic.

Macros per serving (makes 4):

CALORIES	NET CARBS	TOTAL CARBS	FAT	PROTEIN	FIBER
339.3cal	59.3g	63.9g	12.4g	8.1g	4.6g

ORANGE AND CHERRY BISCOTTI

- **2 cups blanched almond flour**
- **¼ cup arrowroot starch or tapioca starch**
- **Zest of 1 orange**
- **⅓ cup maple syrup**
- **½ cup dried unsweetened cherries, chopped**

PANTRY

- **3 tablespoons virgin coconut oil, melted**
- **1 teaspoon vanilla extract**

Dessi has a low-carb version of these biscotti in our keto cookbook, but this version is quite different with the addition of arrowroot starch and maple syrup. The biscotti are perfectly sweet, crunchy, and are begging for a spot of tea or coffee to be dunked in!

Preheat oven to 350°F. Add the almond flour, arrowroot starch, ¼ teaspoon salt, and orange zest to a bowl and mix using a fork.

In a measuring cup or small bowl, add the maple syrup, melted coconut oil, and vanilla extract. Whisk well and pour over the almond flour mixture. Use a fork and mix well. Add the chopped dried cherries and let the dough rest for about 10 minutes. This will allow the almond flour to hydrate.

Place dough on a sheet tray lined with parchment paper. Dip your hands in water and form a 4-inch wide by 10-inch long log. The water will prevent the dough from sticking to your hands. Bake at 350°F for 25 minutes. Remove from oven and transfer dough with parchment paper to a cooling rack for 15 minutes.

Carefully, slice the biscotti log into ¾-inch-wide pieces. Remove the parchment paper and place them on their side, directly onto a cooling rack set in a sheet tray. Bake for 13 to 15 more minutes or until lightly golden brown. Allow to cool and enjoy!

So many **dried cherries** have added sugar and/or sunflower oil. Make sure to read the ingredients and look for one with only one ingredient: cherries!

You can't beat the price of **almond flour** at Costco or Sam's Club. Just keep in mind that almond meal is completely different than almond flour. Stick with flour.

Macros per serving (makes 15):

CALORIES	NET CARBS	TOTAL CARBS	FAT	PROTEIN	FIBER
144.6cal	9.1g	11.2g	10.4g	3.2g	2.1g

I NEVER UNDERSTOOD THE LINK BETWEEN FOOD AND
HEALTH. IT WAS ALWAYS SOMETHING THAT WAS SAID
BUT I DIDN'T FULLY COMPREHEND. I'M ON MY WAY
TO A NORMAL BMI FOR THE FIRST TIME IN ALMOST
EIGHTEEN YEARS BECAUSE OF YOU. I COOK EVERY
SINGLE DAY. I NEVER FEEL DEPRIVED AND HAVE LEARNED
MORE ABOUT FOOD, COOKING, AND NUTRITION
THAN I EVER THOUGHT POSSIBLE! THANK YOU!

–SIERRA M.

PREP TIME: 10 MINUTES • COOKING TIME: 50 MINUTES • MAKES: 6 SERVINGS

PEACH CRISP À LA MODE

- 4 to 5 medium to large organic peaches (or nectarines)
- 1 cup almond flour
- 1 cup organic rolled oats
- 3 tablespoons maple syrup
- 1 pint no-sugar-added ice cream

PANTRY

- 2 teaspoons vanilla extract
- 7 ½ tablespoons grass-fed ghee

There's something very satisfying about making this crisp in a cast iron pan and serving it family style with my favorite sugar-free and dairy-free ice cream. It's easy to make, uses best-in-class ingredients, and everyone is going to love it.

Preheat oven to 350°F. The peaches should be semi-ripe for this recipe. Otherwise they will completely fall apart and be tough to peel if very soft. Peel and slice the peaches into wedges. Place them in a 10-inch cast iron pan with 1 ½ tablespoons of ghee. Cook over medium-low heat until they soften (about 15 to 20 minutes).

Prepare the crisp topping by adding the almond flour, rolled oats, maple syrup, vanilla extract and 6 tablespoons of ghee to a bowl. Use your hands to mix the ingredients and make small clumps. Sprinkle the topping all over the peaches and transfer the cast iron pan into the oven. Bake for about 30 minutes or until the topping is golden brown.

Let cool for a few minutes and top it with ice cream!

You can also make this recipe with **apples**. Buy organic Honeycrisp or Fuji apples, peel, and cook until soft in the cast iron pan. If using apples, I recommend adding one or two of tablespoons of maple syrup to the apples after they cook down to make them a bit sweeter. Also, if you don't feel like peeling the peaches you can skip that part. A little peach fuzz never hurt anyone.

The amount of sugar per serving in most **ice cream** is a bit scary, anywhere from 4 to 7 teaspoons! My favorite is the no-sugar-added line from So Delicious. It's dairy free and has great ingredients except for natural flavors, but it seems most all ice creams do, and I'd rather have that than tons of cane sugar. To learn more, search "FlavCity ice cream" on YouTube.

Always look for **organic oats**; conventional oats tend to score high with the active ingredient in weed killer. Grab a bag of oats for a great price at thrivemarket.com/bobbyapproved, along with other ingredients needed for my recipes and an exclusive offer for FlavCity fans!

Macros per serving (makes 6):

CALORIES	NET CARBS	TOTAL CARBS	FAT	PROTEIN	FIBER	SUGAR ALCOHOLS
451.2cal	29g	40.4g	32.9g	7.7g	9.4g	2g

DOUBLE CHOCOLATE DATE BROWNIES

- 12 ounces of pitted medjool dates (about 2 ½ cups or 15 large dates)
- 4 pasture-raised and organic eggs
- ⅔ cup unsweetened cacao powder
- ¾ cup paleo baking mix (see page 107)
- ½ cup paleo chocolate chips

PANTRY

- 1 cup virgin coconut oil, melted
- 2 teaspoons vanilla extract
- 1 teaspoon baking soda

 Look for **medjool dates** with the pits. They are big, fat, and much juicer than pitted ones.

I am a self-proclaimed brownie aficionado, and I'm telling you that you won't miss the gluten or refined sugar. These brownies are a bit cakey, a bit dense, and I always ask Dessi to make a double batch so we can store some in the freezer.

Preheat oven to 350°F. Soak the dates in very hot water for about 15 minutes. Drain them, but save ¼ cup of the liquid. Add the dates to a food processor (a 7-cup food processor works best) and process until the mixture turns into a smooth paste while adding the reserved ¼ cup of water to it.

Add the eggs one at a time and process until each one gets incorporated into the mixture. Add the melted coconut oil and vanilla and process until it gets incorporated. Add the cacao powder and process again. Add the paleo flour, ½ teaspoon of salt, and 1 teaspoon of baking soda and process for another 20 seconds. Let the mixture rest for 5 minutes so the flour can hydrate.

Pour batter into a 12 x 8 baking pan lined with parchment paper or greased well with coconut oil and dusted with flour. Sprinkle the chocolate chips on top and use a spatula to push them into the mixture a bit.

Bake for about 40 to 45 minutes or until toothpick inserted in the middle comes out clean. Let brownies cool for about 20 minutes, then cut and enjoy! Store in refrigerator for 3 days or freeze for up to 3 months.

If you have never tried Hu Chocolate Gems get ready to be blown away! They are made with organic unrefined coconut sugar, the flavor is fantastic, and I can honestly say I've never seen another **chocolate chip** like this one.

Macros per serving (makes 12):

CALORIES	NET CARBS	TOTAL CARBS	FAT	PROTEIN	FIBER
349cal	26g	29.8g	25.3g	5.4g	3.8g

KETO • PALEO •

IMMUNE-BOOSTING TEA

- 1 lemon
- 2-inch piece of ginger, cut in thin rounds, skin on
- 2-inch piece of turmeric root, cut in thin rounds or grated, skin on
- Tiny pinch of cayenne pepper
- Local honey, preferably raw

PANTRY

- 5 cups of water
- 1 crack of black pepper
- 1 teaspoon virgin coconut oil (or avocado oil)

 I highly encourage you to use fresh **turmeric root** for this recipe, but in a pinch, you can use 1 teaspoon of turmeric powder.

This is one of the most popular recipes on my blog, and when the weather gets cold, it's exactly what the doctor ordered! Be on the lookout for the powdered version of this tea called "FlavCity Immunity Tea," It's my first product ever to hit the market. Just search for it on Google!

Peel the skin from the lemon using a veggie peeler. Add the water, lemon peel, ginger, turmeric, cayenne, and black pepper to a pot and bring to a bare simmer. Then turn the heat down to low and cook for 7 minutes. You don't want the pot to bubble or boil. It's harmful to the nutrients in the turmeric. Take the pot off the heat and squeeze in the juice of a whole lemon and stir in the coconut oil. Strain the tea into a cup and add 1 teaspoon of honey. Enjoy!

The **coconut oil** is needed to help your body absorb the turmeric, and the black pepper activates it. This virgin coconut oil from Thrive Market is the best tasting we have ever tried, and it's regeneratively grown. Grab a tub along with lots of other top-notch groceries needed for my recipes at thrivemarket.com/bobbyapproved, along with an exclusive offer for FlavCity fans.

Macros per serving (makes 5):

CALORIES	NET CARBS	TOTAL CARBS	FAT	PROTEIN	FIBER
31.8cal	6.5g	6.5g	1g	0g	0g

ITALIAN **ALMOND COOKIES**

- · **2 egg whites, pasture-raised and organic**
- · **½ cup maple syrup**
- · **¾ teaspoon almond extract**
- · **2 ¼ cups almond flour**
- · **1 cup sliced almonds, chopped**

PANTRY

- · **½ teaspoon vanilla extract**

 Make sure to buy real-deal **maple syrup**, not the cheap ones made with sugar and caramel coloring. No need to buy organic. I usually buy the big jug at Costco, which happens to be organic anyway!

 My favorite eggs at the store are from Vital Farms, I would get the **pasture-raised and organic eggs** in the orange box.

*These cookies are begging to be dunked in hot coffee, or if you're binging **Last Tango in Halifax** like we are, fancy a kettle? Plus, if you are on team crunch like me, you will love the crispy golden dome of sliced almonds on the outside!*

Preheat oven to 325°F. Place 1 egg white into a medium-size bowl along with the maple syrup and ¼ teaspoon of salt and beat on high with a hand mixer for a couple of minutes until the mixture turns light and fluffy. Add the vanilla extract and almond extract and beat just to combine. Start adding the almond flour, ½ cup at a time, and use a spatula to fold it into the mixture. Once all the flour is incorporated, let the dough rest for 15 minutes, so the almond flour can hydrate. The mixture will be soft and very sticky.

Chop up the sliced almonds into smaller pieces and set aside. Whisk the second egg white, and set it aside. Dip your hands in water and using a cookie dough portion scooper (that is about 1 ½ tablespoons in size) or a spoon, scoop some dough and form it into a ball. The water will prevent the dough from sticking to your hands. Dip the dough ball into the whisked egg white, and then roll it into the chopped up sliced almonds. The egg white will help the almond pieces stick.

Place the balls onto a sheet tray lined with parchment paper. Bake at 325°F for about 30 to 35 minutes until they are deep golden brown around the edges. Let the cookies cool on a wire rack. Store the cookies in a cool dry place.

You can't beat the price of **almond flour** at Costco or Sam's Club. Just keep in mind that almond meal is completely different than almond flour. Stick with flour.

Macros per serving (makes 15):

CALORIES	NET CARBS	TOTAL CARBS	FAT	PROTEIN	FIBER
175.2cal	9g	12.4g	13.3g	6.1g	3.4g

PALEO •

CREAMY HOT COCOA

- 2 tablespoons unsweetened cocoa powder
- 1 ½ tablespoons coconut sugar
- 1 ½ tablespoons coconut milk powder
- ⅓ teaspoon ground cinnamon
- 1 cup 100% grass-fed whole milk (or unsweetened and plain almond milk)

 While most recipes in this book call for raw cacao powder, I find that **cocoa powder** works best for this recipe. It has a stronger flavor because it's baked at high heat and that intensifies the chocolate flavor. Just make sure you buy one that is unsweetened and has no other ingredients.

 Coconut milk powder is shelf stable and can also be used as coffee creamer. Unfortunately, they all seem to have tapioca maltodextrin, which is a preservative, but not as bad as corn-based maltodextrin.

You ain't going to find a mix like this at the grocery store! My version uses coconut sugar, which almost tastes like caramel, and coconut milk powder to make it extra rich and creamy. Whip up a mug and get ready for some binge-watching.

Add the milk to a small pot along with the remaining ingredients and a pinch of salt. Warm over medium heat and whisk very well. If you have a coffee frother, that works best. Grab one at amazon.com/shop/flavcity.

100% grass-fed milk is widely available now, but not always whole milk. 100% grass-fed milk is a good saturated fat with omega-3 fatty acids. There is no reason to get low-fat dairy. Maple Hill and Organic Valley make **100% grass-fed whole milk** that is very high quality. If using almond milk, look for unsweetened and plain. One of the top brands is Malk.

Macros per serving of dry mix, w/o milk added (makes 1):

CALORIES	NET CARBS	TOTAL CARBS	FAT	PROTEIN	FIBER
207.5cal	25.2g	27.6g	8.5g	5g	2.4g

CHOCOLATE AVOCADO PUDDING

- **2 large ripe avocados**
- **Zest of whole orange and ¼ cup of juice**
- **¼ cup hot coffee**
- **½ cup unsweetened cacao powder**
- **½ cup plus 2 tablespoons maple syrup**

PANTRY

- **1 teaspoon vanilla extract**

 Coffee does not need to be organic. The chemicals don't affect the bean, but they do affect the environment and beans are usually grown in the rainforest. If you don't drink coffee, use ¼ cup of strong black tea.

Dessi and I came up with this recipe while living in Venice Beach a few years ago for the winter. The plant-based food scene is epic in LA. This pudding is just as satisfying as the stuff in the grocery store but made with much better ingredients!

Add everything to a blender or food processor along with ¼ teaspoons of salt, then mix on high until smooth and creamy. Check for seasoning and adjust if needed. Will keep in fridge for 2 days.

Cacao is raw and unprocessed. Cocoa is baked at high temperature. Both are good, but I like to use raw cacao for recipes. Just make sure there is no sugar added.

Maple syrup is one of the best paleo sweeteners around. Just make sure it's **real** syrup, not the fake ones made with cane sugar. Grab a jug for a great price at thrivemarket.com/bobbyapproved along with other ingredients needed for my recipes and an exclusive offer for FlavCity fans.

Macros per serving w/o Milk (makes 3):

CALORIES	NET CARBS	TOTAL CARBS	FAT	PROTEIN	FIBER
423.3cal	54.6g	63.3g	20g	7.5g	8.7g

Crispy Baked Chicken
Wings • 155

HAPPY HOUR

PREP TIME: **5 MINUTES** • COOKING TIME: **30 MINUTES** • MAKES: **2 SERVINGS**

CHEESEBURGER AND SWEET POTATO FRIES

- 4 medium-size sweet potatoes
- 1 cup tapioca or arrowroot starch
- Cauliflower sandwich thins
- 12 ounces 100% grass-fed ground beef
- ½ cup 100% grass-fed or organic cheddar cheese, grated

You Tube To see exactly how to make a smash burger, search "FlavCity smash burger" on YouTube.

I love these low-carb and keto-friendly **cauliflower thins** from Outer Aisle, but Trader Joe's has their own version too. I even smear peanut butter on these and eat them as a snack while watching Netflix!

My favorite part of this recipe is the crispy sweet potato fries. I rarely deep fry at home, but these are worth the fuss! If you have not made smash burgers at home, you need to get on that! The meat gets so crusty and caramelized, yummo!

Fill an 8-inch-wide pot with 3 ½ to 4 inches of avocado oil. Alternatively, you could use organic expeller-pressed sunflower or safflower oil, which is a bit less expensive. Preheat over medium heat until the temperature reaches 350°F. Taking the oil temperature is very easy with an infrared thermometer. Grab one at amazon.com/shop/flavcity.

Slice the sweet potatoes into fries, making sure they are not too thick. Add 1 cup of tapioca starch to a large bowl along with ¾ cup of water and whisk well. When the oil is hot, add one handful of fries to the starch water and mix well. Add the fries one at a time. Otherwise they will stick together, Fry for 6 to 8 minutes or until deep golden brown. Once the fries go in the oil, raise the heat just a bit. Fry in very small batches because you don't want to crowd the oil. When the fries are ready, move them to a sheet tray lined with a wire rack and season with salt. Keep warm in the oven and fry the remaining potatoes in batches.

To make the burgers, preheat a large cast iron pan, or even better, a flat cast iron griddle pan over medium-high heat for 3 minutes. Make 4 equal balls from the ground beef and add 1 tablespoon of oil to the griddle. Add the burger balls, and use a heavy spatula to press down as hard as you can to smash them. Immediately season with salt and pepper and let cook until the meat is well caramelized for about 2 to 3 minutes. Flip, season with more salt, pepper, and cover with the grated cheese. Cook for 1 minute more and remove from the heat.

Warm the cauliflower thin buns in the oven according to package instructions. Build the double cheeseburgers and serve with sweet potato fries. Enjoy!

I used quite possibly the best cheese you can buy at the store for this recipe, it's not only 100% grass-fed but also raw! But you can use any **100% grass-fed cheese** you can find, or at least organic.

Macros per serving (makes 2):

CALORIES	NET CARBS	TOTAL CARBS	FAT	PROTEIN	FIBER
1016.5cal	60.7g	70.5g	59g	51.8g	9.8g

Grass-fed beef is available at most grocery stores. Just make sure it says 100% grass-fed or grass-fed and grass-finished, otherwise the cattle are finished on grain, which reverses the health benefits.

WHEN I WAS STARTING MY FITNESS JOURNEY, I STUMBLED

UPON YOUR CHANNEL. MY LIFE DID A 180 FROM THEN

ON! I LOST OVER THIRTY POUNDS FOLLOWING YOUR

COOKBOOK AND FLAVCITY GROCERY SHOPPING! I'M

FEELING BETTER THAN EVER THANKS TO YOU!

–VIVIAN T.

PREP TIME: **2 MINUTES** • COOKING TIME: **10 MINUTES** • MAKES: **2 MARGARITAS**

KETO • PALEO • VEGAN •

SUGAR-FREE MARGARITAS

- **½ cup monk fruit sweetener**
- **2 ounces tequila**
- **¾ ounce fresh lime juice**
- **1 ½ ounces full-fat coconut milk**
- **Pinch of ground cinnamon**

You Tube To watch the video tutorial for this recipe, search "FlavCity margarita" on YouTube.

I used **anejo tequila** for this recipe! I figure this cocktail would cost twenty dollars at a bar, but you can make it at home for three dollars!

I don't drink often, but when I do, I love good tequila, which is why I used top shelf anejo tequila and a monk fruit-based simple syrup to make two darn tasty margaritas that are keto and diabetic friendly!

Make the simple syrup by combining the monk fruit sweetener with ½ cup of filtered water in a small pot. Cook over medium heat until the sugar dissolves, about 6 minutes. Set aside and let cool or add ice cubes if in a hurry. If the syrup begins to crystalize after a while or in the fridge, just warm it up on the burner.

To make the traditional margarita, add a handful of ice along with the tequila, lime juice, and simple syrup to a cocktail shaker. Shake well for 20 seconds and give it a taste. You may want more sweetness. Adjust, shake again, and serve in a glass.

To make the horchata margarita, add ice to a cocktail shaker along with the tequila, lime juice, simple syrup, coconut milk, and cinnamon. Shake well and give it a taste. You may want more sweetness or coconut milk. Adjust, shake well, and serve.

Look for **full-fat coconut milk.** The reduced fat version has more water. Who wants that? Also stick with brands that don't use gums or emulsifiers, like Native Forest (my fave), Thrive Market, or Trader Joe's.

Monk fruit sweetener is my favorite sugar alternative. It's also a one-to-one replacement for white sugar and tastes just like the real thing. Grab the big bag of Lakanto at Costco. It's my favorite brand and the price is unreal!

Macros per serving—Traditional Margarita (makes 2):

CALORIES	NET CARBS	TOTAL CARBS	FAT	PROTEIN	FIBER	SUGAR ALCOHOLS
62.5cal	0.4g	48.8g	0g	0g	0.4g	18g

Macros per serving—Horchata Margarita (makes 2):

CALORIES	NET CARBS	TOTAL CARBS	FAT	PROTEIN	FIBER	SUGAR ALCOHOLS
100cal	1.1g	49.5g	3.4g	0.8g	0.4g	18g

CRISPY BAKED CHICKEN WINGS

- **2 pounds of organic chicken wings and drumettes**
- **½ cup hot sauce**
- **¼ cup grass-fed butter, unsalted**
- **1 cup organic full-fat sour cream**
- **½ large avocado**

PANTRY

- **1 teaspoon baking powder**

You Tube To watch the video tutorial for this recipe, search "FlavCity chicken wings" on YouTube.

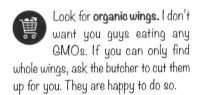

Look for **organic wings.** I don't want you guys eating any GMOs. If you can only find whole wings, ask the butcher to cut them up for you. They are happy to do so.

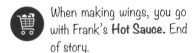

When making wings, you go with Frank's **Hot Sauce.** End of story.

I always use **Kerrygold butter.** It's best to get the silver package that's unsalted, but it's not a big deal if you can only find the salted variety.

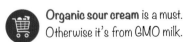

Organic sour cream is a must. Otherwise it's from GMO milk.

The key to getting these wings nice and crispy is chilling them in the fridge and adding a bit of baking powder so the skin dries out. You might notice my recipe calls for twice the amount of butter than most recipes. Trust me, you'll thank me later!

Line a sheet tray with tin foil and place a wire cooling rack inside. Toss the wings with 1 teaspoon of baking powder, arrange in one single layer and place in fridge for 2 hours. The cold air will dry out the chicken skin and help make it really crispy in the oven.

To bake the wings, preheat oven to 400°F and toss the wings with enough avocado oil to coat as well as ½ teaspoons of salt, and arrange back on the wire rack. Bake the wings for 45 minutes. Turn the broiler to medium and cook another 5 to 7 minutes or until the wings turn deep golden brown. Keep your eye on the wings or they will burn. If you have a convection oven, bake at convection at 375°F for the same time and then broil.

While the wings are baking, **make the buffalo sauce** by adding the hot sauce and butter to a small pot and cook over medium-low heat until the butter melts. Whisk well and set aside. If desired, add 1 teaspoon of honey or maple syrup. Make sure to heat the sauce up before tossing with the wings.

Make the avocado dipping sauce by adding the sour cream and avocado to a blender along with ¼ teaspoon of salt and a couple cracks of pepper. Blend well and set aside.

Once the wings come out of the oven, place in a very large bowl, add enough buffalo sauce to coat, and mix well. Add more sauce if needed. Serve wings with leftover buffalo sauce and the avocado dipping sauce, and enjoy!

Macros per serving (makes 2):

CALORIES	NET CARBS	TOTAL CARBS	FAT	PROTEIN	FIBER
1552cal	5.7g	7.9g	131.5g	87.6g	2.3g

I'M SO THANKFUL FOR THE VALUABLE INFORMATION
FROM FLAVCITY ON HOW TO EAT CLEANER. I
DO NOTICE IMPROVEMENTS IN MY OVERALL
HEALTH (LESS TUMMY DISTRESS, MORE ENERGY,
BETTER SLEEP, ETC.). THANK YOU, FLAVCITY!

–MARGARET A.

PREP TIME: **10 MINUTES** • COOKING TIME: **55 MINUTES** • MAKES: **2 SERVINGS**

KETO •

CAULIFLOWER PAN PIZZA

- **1 ½ pounds frozen cauliflower rice, thawed**
- **1 pasture-raised and organic egg**
- **2 ½ cups freshly grated organic mozzarella cheese**
- **½ cup marinara sauce**
- **20 slices of pepperoni**
- **2 teaspoons Italian seasoning**

If you're talking **marinara**, it's Rao's Homemade® all the way. The flavor and ingredients are top notch and you won't find any sugar or processed oils like many sauces on the market. Pro tip—the price at Costco is unbeatable!

Most store-bought cauliflower crusts are loaded with starch or GMO cheeses. Dessi designed this recipe to be really easy to make, and it's perfect when you have a pizza craving on a low-carb diet.

Preheat oven to 450°F or 425°F convection if you have that setting. To make the crust crispy, it's important to squeeze out as much moisture from the thawed cauliflower rice as possible. Once the cauliflower rice is thawed, place it in a kitchen towel, flex those biceps, and squeeze as hard as possible. Try to get every last bit of water out. Add the cauliflower to a blender along with the egg, 1 cup of freshly grated mozzarella cheese, 1 teaspoon salt, a few cracks of pepper, and 2 teaspoons of Italian seasoning if you have it.

Add the dough to a quarter sheet tray lined with parchment paper and flatten the dough so it covers edge to edge. Bake for 20 minutes and remove from oven.

Place a wire cooling rack directly on top of the crust and flip it so the bottom of the crust is now facing up. Remove the parchment paper, place on the wire rack, set inside of a sheet tray, and place back in the oven for about 35 to 45 minutes or until very deep golden-brown color and the edges look very dark.

Remove the crust from the oven, flip it again, but keep it on the cooling rack, top with marinara sauce, 1 ½ cups of cheese, and pepperoni. Bake for another 10 minutes or until cheese is nicely melted.

I know it takes some work to make this crust, but it's worth it! Dessi found a way to make a keto pizza crust that is crispy and holds its shape when topped with sauce and cheese—with only five ingredients!

Cut and serve the pizza, enjoy!

 The reason you want **frozen cauliflower rice** for this recipe is that it's easy to squeeze the water out, something you can't do with fresh. Costco has an amazing deal on a five-pound bag of frozen cauliflower rice!

 I like to buy **block cheese** and grate it myself. The pre-grated stuff does not melt as well and is covered in anti-caking agents like corn starch and wood pulp. Organic is a must when it comes to dairy. 100% grass-fed is even better.

Macros per serving (makes 2):

CALORIES	NET CARBS	TOTAL CARBS	FAT	PROTEIN	FIBER
685cal	16g	24.3g	40.5g	56.5g	8.3g

SUGAR-FREE LEMONADE

- 1 ½ cups monk fruit sweetener
- 4 ½ cups filtered water
- 1 ½ cups freshly squeezed lemon juice, about 10 lemons
- Fresh mint
- Organic blueberries

You Tube To watch the video tutorial for this recipe, search "FlavCity lemonade" on YouTube.

It makes me shiver when I see how much sugar some products contain, especially sweet drinks and soda. Absolutely no one needs 8 teaspoons of cane sugar in one bottle of lemonade or soda. That's a fast track to type 2 diabetes. This diabetic and keto-friendly lemonade tastes just like the real deal, with zero added sugar.

Make the simple syrup. Add the monk fruit and 1 ½ cups of water to a small pot. Cook over medium heat until the sweetener is dissolved, about 5 minutes. Turn heat off under the pot and let cool to room temperature or add some ice if you want to cool it quickly. If the syrup begins to crystalize, just reheat it.

Meanwhile, juice 1 ½ cups of lemon juice in a bowl or pitcher and add 3 cups of water to it. Add 1 cup of the simple syrup and check for seasoning. I find this is the perfect balance, but if you want it sweeter, add the remaining ½ cup of simple syrup. To serve, muddle or smash some blueberries and mint in the bottom of a glass using a fork, pour in some ice, and top with sugar-free lemonade. Enjoy!

Monk fruit sweetener is my favorite sugar alternative. It's also a one-to-one replacement for white sugar, rates a zero on the glycemic index, and tastes just like the real thing. Lakanto classic monk fruit sweetener is always in my pantry, and the big bag at Costco is a fantastic deal!

Blueberries are always on the dirty dozen list, which is why I highly recommend buying organic!

Macros per serving (makes 4):

CALORIES	NET CARBS	TOTAL CARBS	FAT	PROTEIN	FIBER	SUGAR ALCOHOLS
18.8cal	5.5g	53.9g	0g	0.4g	0.4g	48g

HARISSA HUMMUS PLATTER

- **1 red onion**
- **½ pound ground lamb or 100% grass-fed beef**
- **¼ cup harissa sauce**
- **Flatbread**
- **16 ounces hummus**

Why do so many store-bought hummuses use highly processed oils like sunflower or canola?! Look for **hummus** made with extra virgin olive oil, or just make it at home.

Cappello's **naked pizza crust** is the most Bobby Approved crust at the store. It's gluten-free, paleo, and made with top-notch ingredients. If buying a different crust, make sure the wheat is organic and there are no processed oils like soybean, canola, or sunflower.

Talk about serious flavor with minimal ingredients! This recipe utilizes some of the best store-bought ingredients out there. The result is a family-style platter that is monster on flavor with minimal effort.

Preheat oven to 425°F. Make the lamb/beef ragù by finely chopping half of the red onion. Finely slice the other half of the red onion, place in a bowl, and cover with red wine vinegar. Preheat a large nonstick pan just above medium heat with 2 tablespoons of ghee. Add the red onion along with ¼ teaspoon of salt and few cracks of pepper. Cook for 6 minutes and then add the ground lamb/beef. Raise the heat to medium-high, break up the meat, and add ½ a teaspoon of salt and a few cracks of pepper. If you don't have the meat chopper tool I use in all my videos, you are missing out. Grab it on my Amazon shop page: amazon.com/shop/flavcity.

Cook until the meat is almost cooked through, lower the heat to medium-low, and add ¼ cup each of harissa and water. Mix well and cook until the mixture is thick and saucy, about 10 minutes. Check for seasoning after 5 minutes, as you may need more salt or harissa. Spoon out any excess fat that pools at the top. Otherwise it will be too greasy.

Meanwhile, cook the flatbread in the oven for 5 to 6 minutes. Any longer and it will be too hard and crispy. Spread the hummus out on a platter and pour the ragù in the middle. Top with pickled red onions and serve the flatbread on the side. Enjoy!

A lot of people have not tried **harissa**. It's a North African red pepper sauce that has huge flavor and transforms this ragù into something lovely. Look for Mina mild harissa. The ingredients are clean and the flavor is complex.

Macros per serving (makes 2):

CALORIES	NET CARBS	TOTAL CARBS	FAT	PROTEIN	FIBER
1083cal	46.8g	56g	83g	33.5g	9.3g

FLAVCITY HAS TRULY CHANGED MY LIFE. I FOUND FLAVCITY
NOT TOO LONG AGO (NOVEMBER 2019) AND SHORTLY AFTER
I KNEW THAT I WANTED TO TRANSITION TO ORGANIC/GRASS-
FED ITEMS AND I SLOWLY DID IT WITH THE ESSENTIALS PER
BOBBY'S RECOMMENDATIONS (100% GRASS-FED MILK, PASTURE-
RAISED EGGS, GRASS-FED CHEESE, SPROUTED BREAD, ETC.).
THEN READING THE LABELS AND SLOWLY TRANSITIONING
ALL. I CAN HAPPILY SAY THAT I AM 85 TO 90% ORGANIC/GRASS-
FED AND IT HAS MADE ME FEEL INCREDIBLE. I DON'T EVEN
REMEMBER THE LAST TIME I HAD TO TAKE ANY MEDICINE AND
I FEEL THE HEALTHY FOOD I AM PUTTING IN MY BODY IS A
HUGE PART OF IT. I AM FOREVER A FAN AND SUPPORTER, AND
WILL BE FOREVER GRATEFUL TO FLAVCITY! I LOVE YOU GUYS!

–ELSY R.

I FOUND YOUR CHANNEL AND HAVE LEARNED SO MUCH ABOUT CLEAN EATING. I CLEANED OUT MY CABINETS OF WHITE FLOUR AND THE DEVIL. I ORDERED YOUR BOOK AND SOMEHOW GOT TWO. TWO WEEKS LATER MY DIABETIC FRIEND ASKED FOR KETO RECIPES ON FACEBOOK. I TEXTED HER THAT I HAD THE BOOK SHE NEEDED. I DOWNLOADED YOUR APP AND USE IT WHEN I GO TO THE GROCERY STORE. THANK YOU FOR THE CHANNEL AND SHARING YOUR FAMILY AND ART.

–JANET Y.

KALE AND CAULIFLOWER SALAD

- **7 ounces organic Lacinato/ Tuscan kale**
- **½ a large head of cauliflower**
- **1 cup walnuts**
- **½ cup finely grated parmesan cheese**
- **1 lemon**
- **¼ cup organic raisins**

If you follow me on YouTube, I often talk about gut-friendly foods. This recipe is your gut's new BFF because it's loaded with prebiotic fiber, which feed your gut bacteria. It's also incredibly easy to make but so darn satisfying.

Roast the walnuts on a sheet tray in a 300°F oven for about 15 to 20 minutes or until golden brown. Roughly chop and set aside.

Grate the cauliflower using the largest setting on a box grater and add to a large bowl. Wash and dry the kale leaves and strip the leaves from the stalk. If you want to see a really cool hack to strip the kale, search "FlavCity summer food hacks" on YouTube.

Finely chop the kale and add it to the bowl with the riced cauliflower. Add the cheese, almost all the walnuts, a good pinch of salt, a few cracks of pepper, 3 ½ tablespoons of extra virgin olive oil, the zest of half a lemon, and the juice of 1 lemon. Also add the raisins if you have them. Mix well and check for seasoning as you may need more cheese or lemon juice. Serve the salad and top with reserved walnuts and grate over more cheese. Enjoy!

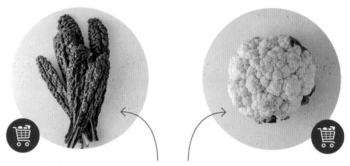

Kale should always be bought organic. It's one of the dirtiest of the dirty dozen. Stick with Lacinato kale. It's also called black, Tuscan, or dinosaur. It's much more tender and pleasant to eat than green curly kale! Cauliflower is on the clean fifteen list, no need to buy organic.

Macros per serving (makes 2):

CALORIES	NET CARBS	TOTAL CARBS	FAT	PROTEIN	FIBER
782cal	20.5g	31.9g	66.2g	23g	11.4g

BBQ PULLED PORK TAQUITOS

- **2 pounds pasture-raised pork shoulder, boneless**
- **1 ¼ cup no-added-sugar BBQ sauce**
- **12 tortillas**
- **20 ounces tomatillos**
- **½ large avocado**

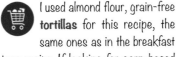

I used almond flour, grain-free **tortillas** for this recipe, the same ones as in the breakfast taco recipe. If looking for corn-based tortillas, make sure they are organic or at least non-GMO. Check out the tortillas I used in the Breakfast Tacos recipe (page 54).

Have you read the ingredients on most BBQ sauces? Yikes! Tons of added sugar, caramel coloring, and preservatives. Look for Primal Kitchen **BBQ sauce.** Their Hawaiian or mango jalapeño BBQ sauce is so tasty with best-in-class ingredients.

*This is serious, clean eating, Tex-Mex comfort food! Tender pulled pork, crispy tortillas, paleo BBQ sauce, and a roasted tomatillo avocado salsa all made with only five ingredients. **Dios mio!***

To cook the pork shoulder, cut it into 4 equal pieces roughly the size of your fist. Season the pork pieces all over with a pinch of salt and pepper. Preheat an electric or stove-top pressure cooker to high along with 2 tablespoons of avocado oil. Sear the pork on all sides until deep golden brown for about 10 minutes. This step is optional, but it does add caramelized yummy flavor to the pork.

Add 1 cup of BBQ sauce to the pot along with ¾ cup of water. The liquid should cover about ¾ of the pork. Seal the pressure cooker and pressure cook on high for 45 minutes. When ready, turn the pot off and let it sit for 10 minutes, then carefully release the pressure.

If you don't have a pressure cooker, I would highly recommend getting one, but not just for this recipe since we use it all the time on FlavCity Instagram stories for dinner. See my recommendations at amazon.com/shop/flavcity. Otherwise you can cook the pork in a slow cooker on high for 6 to 7 hours following the same steps to sear the pork in a cast iron pan. Or you can cook it in a Dutch oven for 2 hours with the lid closed over a very gentle simmer.

Allow the pork to rest for 10 minutes once it comes out of the pot. Then use two forks to finely shred it. Add a bit of cooking liquid to the pork to keep it moist.

While to pork is cooking, **make the tomatillo sauce** by preheating the broiler to medium. Peel the tomatillos, season with a shot of avocado oil, a pinch of salt, couple cracks of pepper, and broil until very soft and blistered for about 8 to 10 minutes. Place the tomatillos in a blender along with the avocado, a pinch of salt, and a couple cracks of pepper. Blend until smooth and creamy and check for seasoning. A ½ teaspoon of honey or maple syrup would balance the acidity if you have it! Set aside.

Warm the tortillas directly on a burner or wrap in wet paper towels and place in microwave for 15 seconds. Add 2 to 3 tablespoons of the pork filling to each tortilla, wrap tight, and place 1 to 2 toothpicks through to keep them closed.

Macros per serving (makes 3):

CALORIES	NET CARBS	TOTAL CARBS	FAT	PROTEIN	FIBER
1510.3cal	67.9g	77g	96.6g	80.6g	9.1g

Pasture-raised pork is almost impossible to find at the grocery store. To find local farms and markets that sell pasture pork, chicken, and more, go to eatwild.com and search by your zip code.

Preheat air fryer to 400°F, spray the basket with avocado oil, and spray the taquitos with oil on all sides. Air fry for 8 to 10 minutes, flipping halfway if needed, remove, and fry the rest. Keep taquitos warm in the oven. If baking in the oven, place taquitos on a wire rack set inside a sheet tray, spray well, and bake at 425°F for 15 to 20 minutes or until golden brown. Of course, you could deep fry them in avocado oil too!

Serve the taquitos with the tomatillo sauce and extra BBQ sauce. Enjoy!

FLAVCITY CHANGED MY WHOLE WORLD! LEARNING ABOUT WHAT I'M ACTUALLY PUTTING IN MY BODY HAS BEEN INVALUABLE TO MY HEALTH AND MY JOURNEY TO LIVING A MORE HOLISTIC LIFESTYLE. BOBBY, DESSI, AND TEAM HAVE SUCH AMAZING ONLINE CONTENT AND THEIR FIRST BOOK WAS SO DELICIOUS TO COOK THROUGH. CAN'T WAIT TO SEE WHAT ELSE THEY HAVE IN STORE FOR US!

–NIKITA N.

BRAZILIAN **CHEESY POPOVERS**

- 1 pasture-raised and organic egg
- 1 cup grass-fed milk, full fat
- ½ cup avocado oil
- 1 cup freshly grated parmesan cheese
- 1 ½ cups sour tapioca starch

My Brazilian buddy Sergio taught me this recipe many years ago. You've probably had Pão de Queijo at one of those all-you-can-eat Brazilian steakhouses. This version is easy. Just mix in a blender, bake, and watch them rise sky high in the oven.

Preheat oven to 400°F. Add the egg, milk, oil, and cheese to a blender and mix on high for 10 seconds. Add ¼ teaspoon baking powder, 1 teaspoon salt, put the lid on, and blend at medium speed. With the motor running, add the sour tapioca starch, one large spoonful at a time. Once all the starch is in, mix on high for 10 seconds.

Lightly spray a nonstick popover tin or a mini muffin tin with avocado oil and fill the tins halfway with the batter. Bake for 23 to 25 minutes or until golden brown. Remove from heat and let the rolls sit in the tins for a few minutes as they deflate a bit.

Enjoy!

You really want to use **sour tapioca starch** to make this recipe authentically Brazilian. Go to amazon.com/shop/flavcity to get the one we used (polvilho azedo). If you don't want to buy it, you can use regular tapioca starch, but it won't be quite the same.

There are some really great **100% grass-fed milk** options at the store now. Maple Hill and Organic Valley are just a couple, even ALDI has one. It's not whole milk but will still work. Organic whole milk would be the next best, but I would not use conventional GMO milk.

My favorite eggs at the store are from Vital Farms. I would get the **pasture-raised and organic eggs** in the orange box.

Macros per serving (makes 16):

CALORIES	NET CARBS	TOTAL CARBS	FAT	PROTEIN	FIBER
139.9cal	11.2g	11.2g	9.4g	3.3g	0g

BOBBY, YOU'VE CHANGED HOW I SHOP FOR, COOK, AND VIEW FOOD. THE VIDEOS EMPOWERED ME TO FIND THE BEST INGREDIENTS AFFORDABLY AND THE RECIPES TAUGHT ME EXCITING WAYS TO USE THEM. I AM FOREVER GRATEFUL. ALSO, I RAN INTO YOU IN WHOLE FOODS ONE TIME AND YOU WERE INCREDIBLY GRACIOUS WHEN MY GIRLFRIEND TOLD YOU THAT YOUR DAUGHTER'S NAME MADE HER CRY. SO, THANKS FOR THAT TOO.

–GRANT Z.

PREP TIME: **5 MINUTES** • INACTIVE COOKING TIME: **75 MINUTES** • COOKING TIME: **25 MINUTES** • MAKES: **4 SERVINGS**   PALEO • VEGAN •

ROASTED BEET HUMMUS

- **2 pounds beets**
- **¼ cup tahini**
- **¾ teaspoon cumin**
- **3 cloves garlic**
- **Zest of half lemon, juice of whole lemon**

I could have made this recipe with chickpeas, but where's the fun in that? Roasted beets have such a lovely flavor, plus it looks super cool and more nutrient dense than chickpeas. Dessi is huge fan of this recipe! She loves to smear it on some toasted pita bread or dip raw veggies in it as a snack.

Preheat oven to 400°F and place the beets in a roasting dish with ¼ cup of water. Cover dish with tinfoil, place the garlic cloves that are still in their paper on top of the foil, and place in the oven. Remove the garlic after 15 minutes and bake the beets for a total of 75 minutes. The beets are ready when a thin knife goes in and out with relative ease.

Once the beets have cooled a bit, use paper towels to peel the skin off. I like to wear food-safe gloves for this.

Once peeled, add beets to a blender along with all the tahini, cumin, lemon zest and juice, garlic, ½ teaspoon salt, and a couple cracks of pepper. Blend on high until smooth and creamy. Check for seasoning as you may need more salt or lemon juice.

Serve and enjoy!

Tahini is very underrated in the USA. It's the sesame seed version of peanut butter and has such a lovely nutty and bitter flavor. My favorite is made by Mighty Sesame Co. They source really good Ethiopian seeds and the flavor is great. Just remember, tahini should always be runny and pourable. Otherwise, if it's too thick, it's very bitter.

Macros per serving (makes 4):

CALORIES	NET CARBS	TOTAL CARBS	FAT	PROTEIN	FIBER
338.5cal	21.2g	25.8g	22.8g	8.5g	4.6g

UNDER THE SEA-FOOD

PALEO •

SWEET AND STICKY SHRIMP CAKES

- 2 pounds wild shrimp, peeled and cleaned
- ½ cup avocado oil mayonnaise
- ½ cup maple syrup
- 1 to 2 teaspoons sriracha sauce
- Juice of 1 lime

Always buy **wild shrimp!** Shrimp farming is notorious for being really dirty and we have an abundance of wild-caught Gulf of Mexico shrimp in the USA. Frozen shrimp are fine too. Just make sure to thaw overnight in the fridge.

When buying **avocado oil mayo,** make sure there is no sugar added or other oils in the ingredients. Many products will say avocado or olive oil on the front, but if you read the ingredients you will see canola or soybean oil. Very tricky, but they can't fool us!

Everyone loves a bottle of sweet chili sauce from the grocery store, but have you looked at the ingredients? High fructose corn syrup, cane sugar, and other nasty stuff I don't want you putting in your body. Make my homemade version of this sauce and drizzle it all over these juicy shrimp cakes.

Make the shrimp cakes by adding the shrimp to a blender or food processor along with ½ cup of mayonnaise, 1 ½ teaspoons of salt, and a few cracks of pepper. Blend until fairly smooth, but still a bit chunky monkey.

To cook the cakes, preheat a large nonstick pan over medium-high heat for 3 minutes with enough avocado oil to coat the bottom of the pan. Wet your hands, grab ¼ cup of mixture, flatten with your hands and add to the pan. Try to make the cakes on the thin side. Add four cakes total to the pan, cook until deep golden brown on the first side for about 3 minutes, flip and cook another 2 minutes. Remove and keep warm. Cook the remaining cakes adding more oil to the pan if needed.

Make the sweet sticky sauce. Once all the shrimp cakes are cooked, keep them warm and carefully wipe out all of the oil. Add the maple syrup, sriracha, and the juice of half a lime to the pan and turn the heat just above medium. Cook for a few minutes or until the sauce has reduced a bit and thickened. Check for seasoning but be careful because the sauce is really hot! You may need more lime juice. Adjust according to your taste. Pour the sauce over the shrimp cakes and enjoy!

Many **sriracha** brands have preservatives added like potassium sorbate and sodium bisulfite, which should be avoided. I really like Sky Valley® Sriracha. The ingredients are top notch and the fermented chili flavor is yummo!

Macros per serving (makes 3):

CALORIES	NET CARBS	TOTAL CARBS	FAT	PROTEIN	FIBER
763.3cal	40g	40.1g	43.7g	54.1g	0.1g

SALMON COBB SALAD

- Two 5-ounce salmon filets
- 3-pack organic romaine hearts
- 4 pieces organic or pasture-raised bacon
- 2 pasture-raised and organic eggs
- Ranch dressing

You have to be very selective when buying farm-raised **salmon**, which is why I really like Mowi Salmon. Their farming practices are top notch, the salmon is loaded with omega-3 fatty acids, and it's much harder to overcook compared to wild. You can find Mowi on Amazon fresh. To learn more, search "FlavCity seafood guide" on YouTube.

My favorite lunches tend to be on the lighter side. A good salad with a quality piece of protein on top is right up my alley. This recipe utilizes top-notch, store-bought salad dressings and a few techniques to make a simple salad with monster flavors.

Make the eggs by bringing a medium size pot of water to a boil, add the eggs, and cook exactly 11 minute. Remove the eggs, place back in the empty pot, and run cold water over the eggs for 2 minutes. Gently crack the shells in a few spots while the water is running. This will make them easier to peel. After 2 minutes, gently crack the egg all over on a cutting board and roll it. Place the eggs under running water and peel the shell away. The water will make this process much easier.

Meanwhile, **cook the bacon** on a sheet tray in a 400°F oven for 15 minutes or until crispy. Remove from oven, roughly chop, and set aside.

To make the salmon, first dry the salmon fillets with a paper towel, especially the skin side. Preheat a medium-size nonstick pan over medium-high heat with 1 tablespoon of avocado oil. Once hot, season the salmon with salt and pepper on all sides and place skin side down in the pan. Let cook until the skin is deep golden brown for about 5 to 6 minutes, turn the heat down to medium-low, and flip the salmon. Cook for 3 minutes and then turn the salmon on both sides for 30 seconds each. Remove from the heat, and just to make sure it's cooked to your liking, cut into a piece.

Roughly chop 2 to 3 of the romaine hearts and add to a large bowl with ¼ teaspoon of salt, a few cracks of pepper, and the chopped bacon. Pour over some dressing and toss well.

To serve, break up or flake the salmon on top of the lettuce along with some sliced eggs. Enjoy!

95% of the **salad dressings** sold at the store are garbage! They're loaded with processed GMO oils, added sugar, preservatives, and more. Look for ones made with avocado or olive oil and no added sugars. Search "FlavCity salad dressing" on YouTube to learn more.

Macros per serving (makes 2):

CALORIES	NET CARBS	TOTAL CARBS	FAT	PROTEIN	FIBER
823.5cal	7.4g	10.9g	65.8g	48.4g	3.5g

CRUNCHY **SHRIMP TACOS**

- 1 pound wild-caught shrimp, peeled and cleaned
- 2 tablespoons taco seasoning mix
- 1 cup store-bought salsa
- 12-ounce bag slaw mix
- Hard shell tacos
- Avocado oil mayonnaise

Siete brand is one of my favorites, and their **taco seasoning mix** uses next level ingredients. If buying another brand, avoid added sugar, corn meal, MSG, or preservatives.

Why have I been sleeping on hard shell tacos the last twenty years!? Crunchy paleo taco shells filled with tangy slaw, crusty shrimp, and the most delightful buttery pan salsa you could imagine. **Que rico, amigos!**

Season the shrimp with 1 teaspoon of oil, 2 tablespoons of taco seasoning, mix well, and let sit at room temperature. Hold off on adding the salt as you don't want to draw moisture out of the shrimp.

Make the slaw by adding the slaw mix to a bowl and seasoning with ½ teaspoon salt, a few cracks of pepper, 3 tablespoons extra virgin olive oil, and 1 ½ tablespoons red wine vinegar. Use your hands to really rough up and mix the salad. If will taste better if it sits for 20 minutes. If you have avocado oil mayonnaise, skip the olive oil and use 3 to 4 tablespoons directly into the slaw along with the vinegar and mix well. The creaminess goes very well with the tacos.

To cook the shrimp, preheat a large cast iron pan over medium-high heat for 3 minutes. A nonstick pan works too. Add 2 tablespoons of ghee to the pan and 1 teaspoon of salt to the shrimp. Mix the shrimp well and only add half to the pan. Cook for 3 minutes undisturbed, flip and only cook 1 minute more. Remove from the pan and cook the second batch. You will want a splatter guard for this. Go to amazon.com/shop/flavcity to get one; you will thank me later.

Once the second batch of shrimp are done, remove from the pan and lower heat to medium. Add ½ cup of water, and let it reduce for 1 minute, then add 1 cup of salsa. Allow the sauce to reduce in half, about 5 minutes. Reduce heat to low, add 1 tablespoon of ghee, and mix well. Roughly chop the shrimp and add to the pan, mix well, and coat the shrimp in the buttery salsa.

Warm the hard shell tacos in the oven according to package instructions. I like to put some slaw in the bottom of the shell, top with shrimp, and extra salsa. Enjoy!

Avoid any store-bought salsa with added sugar or tomato puree. My favorite is Frontera brand double-smoked **tomato salsa.** I have yet to find a better tasting salsa.

→

Macros per serving (makes 3):

CALORIES	NET CARBS	TOTAL CARBS	FAT	PROTEIN	FIBER
540cal	28.3g	35.7g	32.8g	30.7g	7.3g

There are two **corn-free paleo hard shell tacos** I love. One is from Thrive Market and the other one is Siete. They both use avocado oil. If you want corn tortillas, hard or soft, go with organic or non-GMO corn. Grab all the groceries needed for my recipes for cheaper than the grocery store at thrivemarket.com/bobbyapproved, along with an exclusive offer for FlavCity fans!

Always buy **wild shrimp!** Shrimp farming is notorious for being really dirty and we have an abundance of wild-caught Gulf of Mexico shrimp in the USA. Frozen shrimp are fine too. Just make sure to thaw overnight in the fridge.

If you buy any slaw mix that has **kale** in it, make sure it's organic. Otherwise, **red or green cabbage** can be conventional since they are on the clean fifteen list.

SALMON PATTIES AND TARTAR SAUCE

- 2 pounds wild salmon, skin removed and cubed
- ⅔ cup avocado oil mayonnaise
- 2 teaspoons stone-ground mustard
- ¾ cup almond flour
- Tartar sauce

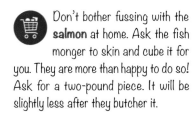

Don't bother fussing with the **salmon** at home. Ask the fish monger to skin and cube it for you. They are more than happy to do so! Ask for a two-pound piece. It will be slightly less after they butcher it.

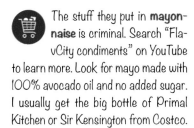

The stuff they put in **mayonnaise** is criminal. Search "FlavCity condiments" on YouTube to learn more. Look for mayo made with 100% avocado oil and no added sugar. I usually get the big bottle of Primal Kitchen or Sir Kensington from Costco.

Almond flour is not the same as almond meal. Costco has the best price along with Sam's club.

Usually fish cakes are made with starchy breadcrumbs for a binder, mayonnaise that is made with highly processed GMO oils, and topped with tartar sauce with ingredients that would make you shiver in your boots! This recipe is the opposite, and I found the best store-bought tartar sauce that has ever graced the supermarket.

Add the almond flour to a small bowl and add just enough water to make wet and mushy. Allow to sit for 3 minutes.

Add the salmon to a food processor or blender with the mayo, mustard, almond flour mixture, 1 ½ teaspoons salt, and a few cracks of pepper. Mix on high until smooth but still with a few chunks here and there.

Preheat a large nonstick pan over medium-high heat with enough avocado oil to coat the bottom of the pan. Wait for the oil to get hot, wet your hands, scoop ¼ cup of the salmon mixture, flatten a bit, add to pan, and carefully press the patty down and make it thinner. Add 4 patties to the pan and cook until deep golden for about 4 to 5 minutes. Flip and cook another 3 minutes. Remove from pan and keep warm, cook remaining salmon patties.

Serve the salmon patties with tartar sauce and enjoy!

Primal Kitchen makes a **tartar sauce** that Dessi is not only addicted to but also the ingredients are fantastic! I can't find another clean brand on the market because they all use processed oils like canola, added sugar, and other nasty stuff.

Macros per serving (makes 3):

CALORIES	NET CARBS	TOTAL CARBS	FAT	PROTEIN	FIBER
1222cal	2.9g	6.4g	100.3g	71.3g	3.5g

LAZY-A$$ TUNA SALAD

- **Two 5-ounce tins of chunk light/ skipjack tuna packed in water**
- **½ cup avocado oil mayonnaise**
- **2 teaspoons stone ground mustard**
- **Juice of 1 lemon**
- **¾ cup celery, finely sliced**

The stuff they put in **mayonnaise** is criminal. Search "FlavCity condiments" on YouTube to learn more. Look for mayo made with 100% avocado oil and no added sugar. I usually get Primal Kitchen or Chosen Foods.

This is my go-to lunch during busy weekdays. It's called lazy because you just dump, stir, and voila, it's done! But this tuna salad is made with some of the best ingredients you can buy and is way better than any pre-made version from the deli counter.

Drain the tuna well and add to a large bowl with the remaining ingredients, ¼ teaspoon salt, and a few cracks of pepper. Mix very well and check for seasoning. You may need a touch more mayonnaise. Don't forget my favorite part of the celery—the leaves! Finely chop and add to the salad. This tuna salad gets even better the next day!

The larger the tuna, the more mercury it has, which is why I avoid albacore and look for **chunk light or skipjack tuna**. I also look for "pole & line"-caught tuna. That's the responsible way to fish instead of dragging a net through the sea and killing other creatures. Get a great price on tuna and lots of other ingredients needed for my recipes at thrivemarket.com/bobbyapproved along with an exclusive offer!

Macros per serving (makes 3):

CALORIES	NET CARBS	TOTAL CARBS	FAT	PROTEIN	FIBER
357.3cal	1.7g	2.1g	30.3g	18.8g	0.4g

IT'S ALL ABOUT THAT BROTH

RED THAI SCALLOP SOUP

- Mirepoix (see page 28)
- ¼ cup red curry paste
- 1 can full-fat coconut milk
- 1 quart beef bone broth
- 12 ounces bay scallops
- Lime juice

Always have a jar or two of **red curry paste** in your pantry. What a flavor bomb!

Bay scallops can be bought frozen. It won't matter for this recipe. If you need to defrost them in a hurry, run under cold water in a colander.

Who makes meatballs out of scallops? This guy! Trust me, the sweet and briny flavor of the scallops infuse into the broth and give it a seafood bisque-like flavor. You can also do this with shrimp, and the soup gets even better the second day!

Preheat a large soup pot over medium heat with 2 tablespoons of ghee. Add the mirepoix along with ½ teaspoon of salt and a few cracks of pepper. Cook for 15 minutes or until the veggies are very soft. Add the curry paste, cook for 2 minutes, and then add the bone broth. Add 1 teaspoon of salt and bring the broth to a gentle simmer. Cover the pot and cook for 35 minutes.

Meanwhile, **make the meatballs** by placing the scallops in a food processor or blender with ¾ teaspoon salt and a few cracks of pepper. Blend until smooth and sticky for about 6 seconds.

After the soup has cooked for 20 minutes, check for seasoning since it will most likely need more salt. After 35 minutes take the lid off and turn the heat down to the lowest setting. Use two spoons to form small meatballs with the scallop mixture. It will look more like mini footballs. Once all of the meatballs are in the broth, cook uncovered for 5 minutes. The heat from the broth will gently cook the meatballs.

If you have a lime, squeeze the juice of half a lime in the pot and turn off the heat. Serve and enjoy!

Bone broth is one of my secret weapons, not just for cooking but for gut health! Kettle & Fire bone broth is one of the best one you can find at the store. They use 100% grass-fed and finished bones and the quality is top notch. If you are not going to make the homemade version on page 200, get a couple boxes of this bone broth.

Macros per serving (makes 3):

CALORIES	NET CARBS	TOTAL CARBS	FAT	PROTEIN	FIBER
507.7cal	12.2g	13.6g	33.7g	31.4g	1.4g

LENTIL CURRY STEW

- Mirepoix (see page 28)
- ¼ cup red curry paste
- 1 heaping cup organic red split lentils
- 1 quart beef bone broth
- ½ bunch organic Lacinato kale

I've become obsessed with one-pot wonders made in my Le Creuset pot. I've made this stew many times, but usually with much more ingredients. I was stoked to see how beautiful the flavor was with only five ingredients. The kicker is bone broth. I can't stress enough how important it is for this recipe and the others in this book!

Preheat a soup pot over medium heat with 2 tablespoons of ghee. Add the mirepoix along with ½ teaspoon of salt and a few cracks of pepper. Cook for 15 minutes or until the veggies are very soft. Add the curry paste, rinse the lentils in cold water, and add those to the pot. Cook for 2 minutes and then add the bone broth. Bring to a gentle simmer and put the lid on the pot and cook for 35 minutes, checking for seasoning after 20 minutes. The stew will likely need more salt.

Meanwhile, remove the stems from the kale and roughly chop. During the last 5 minutes of cook time, add the kale. Turn the heat off the pot and check for seasoning one last time. Serve and enjoy!

Kale should always be bought organic, it's one of the dirtiest of the dirty dozen. Stick with Lacinato kale; it's also called black, Tuscan, or dinosaur. It's much more tender and pleasant to eat than green curly kale!

I would always buy organic beans and **lentils**. Otherwise they can have high levels of weed killer. Split lentils cook really fast and they are loaded with fiber and protein. Scoop some along with lots of other groceries needed for my recipes at thrivemarket.com/bobbyapproved.

This **red curry paste** is an absolute flavor bomb. I always have this in my fridge for big flavors with no effort required.

Macros per serving (makes 3):

CALORIES	NET CARBS	TOTAL CARBS	FAT	PROTEIN	FIBER
440.7cal	30.2g	54g	10.2g	33.2g	23.8g

ITALIAN **WEDDING SOUP**

- Mirepoix (see page 28)
- 1 ½ cups marinara sauce
- 1 quart beef bone broth
- 12 ounces organic ground turkey thigh meat
- 4 ounces organic red lentil pasta

If you're talking **marinara**, it's Rao's Homemade® all the way. The flavor and ingredients are top notch!

Red lentil pasta could be one of my favorite inventions! Not only is it gluten free, but it's made with nutrient-dense lentil, not simple starches like most gluten-free pasta is. There are so many top-quality pasta and pantry options at thrivemarket.com/bobbyapproved, along with an exclusive offer just for my fans!

*So much flavor in this one-pot wonder from only five ingredients! I can't begin to tell you how important bone broth is for this recipe. It adds so much body and flavor! Combine that with some Rao's Homemade®, mini meatballs, and lentil pasta, and this soup is **nonna** approved.*

Preheat a large soup pot over medium heat with 2 tablespoons of ghee. Add the mirepoix along with ½ teaspoon of salt and a few cracks of pepper. Cook for 15 minutes or until the veggies are very soft. Add the marinara sauce, cook for 1 minute, and then add the bone broth. Season with another ½ teaspoon of salt, bring to a gentle simmer, then place a lid on the pot and cook for 35 minutes.

Meanwhile, **boil the red lentil rotini pasta** according to box instructions and set aside.

To make the meatballs, season the ground turkey meat with ¾ teaspoon salt and a few cracks of pepper. Mix well and form mini meatballs, but first get your hands wet so the mixture does not stick. Shout-out to my mother-in-law for that gem of a tip!

Check the soup for seasoning after 20 minutes as it will most likely need more salt. After 35 minutes, remove the lid and turn the heat down a notch. Add the mini meatballs and cook for 8 minutes. Cut one of the meatballs in half to make sure they are cooked through.

Add the cooked pasta, serve, and enjoy!

Organic ground turkey is a must. Otherwise it's fed a strict diet of GMO grains. Most packs don't label the turkey as "dark meat" or "thighs," but the color is noticeably darker than the breast meat and it won't say 99% lean meat on the package.

Macros per serving (makes 3):

CALORIES	NET CARBS	TOTAL CARBS	FAT	PROTEIN	FIBER
540.7cal	27.6g	34g	28.2g	38.1g	6.4g

PREP TIME: **2 MINUTES** • COOKING TIME: **3 HOURS** • MAKES: **3 QUARTS**

KETO • PALEO •

NOURISHING BEEF BONE BROTH

- 3 pounds assorted grass-fed beef bones
- 2 stalks celery, cleaned and halved
- 2 large carrots, cleaned and halved
- 1 onion, quartered with the skin on

PANTRY

- ½ cup red wine or 1 ½ tablespoons raw apple cider vinegar
- Filtered water

 Where to find **grass-fed bones?** Good luck finding them at the store. Instead get them from a company that a FlavCity fan started, shepherdmeats.com. Order the knuckle, neck, and marrow bones if they have them. Use FLAVCITY for 15% off, and their grass-fed Tasmanian beef is heavenly.

When you only have five ingredients, you'd better make them count! I would venture to say bone broth is the most important ingredient in this book, and when you make it at home it's so economical compared to buying at the store. Loaded with collagen, gelatin, and chondroitin, it's not only yummy but great for your gut, joints, and skin!

Roast the bones for 10 minutes at 400°F on a sheet tray in the oven. For a gelatinous and nutrient-dense broth, use a combination of bones like knuckle, neck, and marrow bones. Place all ingredients in the instant pot or pressure cooker along with 10 black peppercorns and fill with enough water to just cover the bones. Soak the bones for 30 minutes. The acid in the wine or vinegar will help draw out minerals from the bones. Add some more water to reach the maximum line in the pressure cooker and pressure cook on high for 3 hours. Carefully release the pressure. I take the pot outside to do this, so the kitchen doesn't smell like a barn. Strain the broth and save bones for another use. Let cool to room temperature. You may have to wait overnight. Store in fridge for 7 days or freeze for 6 months.

Once cooled, you need to remove the fat layer on top of the broth. You can use it for cooking or toss it away. To serve, warm a cup and add a pinch of good sea salt. Enjoy!

Make another batch with the same bones and add one fresh roasted bone to the pot. You can do this a third time too if you have fridge space! The cost per gallon comes down to around five dollars compared with forty dollars per gallon for store-bought. Winning!

I always use raw **apple cider vinegar** with the mother. It has living probiotic bacteria that are fantastic for the gut. You can add a shot to a cup of water and start your day off on the right foot or use it for salad dressings.

Macros for 3 quarts:

CALORIES	NET CARBS	TOTAL CARBS	FAT	PROTEIN	FIBER
450cal	0g	0g	0g	115g	0g

My goal is to make you a master in the kitchen and the grocery store. We have tons of information in this cookbook and even more on the *FlavCity* YouTube, Instagram, and Facebook pages, and our blog, but we just came out with the Bobby Approved app!

The app is your ultimate shopping companion. Not only does it have all of the information from every video we have ever made, but it also has a bar code scanner feature. You can scan any bar code in the grocery store and the app will tell you if it's Bobby Approved or not, and why. It's as if I am shopping with you to help you buy the best products for you and your family. You can also browse the app to learn about any aisle of the grocery store and how to buy the best products.

I really believe this app will make you a better shopper, allow you to get in and out of the store faster, and leave you feeling empowered to know that you are buying the best stuff the grocery store has to offer. Search for the Bobby Approved app in the Apple App Store or on Google Play.

Our first cookbook, *Keto Meal Prep by FlavCity*, is still a #1 bestseller on Amazon after a year and a half! The amount of positive feedback we have heard from fans has been unreal. Every single day I read a comment or email from someone who has lost weight or been able to reduce their medications because of the keto diet and the information I put on the *FlavCity* YouTube channel. If you are looking for moderate-fat, low-carb keto recipes with monster flavor, I would highly recommend checking out this cookbook, our FlavCity *YouTube* channel, and flavcity.com for tons of free recipes.

Keto Meal Prep
by flavcity

125+
LOW CARB RECIPES
THAT ACTUALLY
taste good

BOBBY PARRISH & DESSI PARRISH

THANK YOU

I've been making YouTube videos for over eight years now, and the only reason I've been successful and been able to make a career out of this is because of the FlavCity community. Over 2.4 million FlavCity family members support our community online, and I call them family because I know many of them and they share my content with friends, family, and coworkers. We live in a society of swipe left, swipe up, and scroll down, but something is different with FlavCity fans. They really care about me and my family and want to help spread the word about FlavCity. Whether you have been with us the whole time or just found our videos thanks to some algorithm, I want to say thank you for letting me do this for a living and allowing me to turn my passion for shopping and cooking into something I get to do every day!

We are a small crew over here at FlavCity HQ, a.k.a. our two-bedroom condo in Chicago. Big thanks to my wife Dessi and my good pal Art. It's amazing how much content we have created among us. I love sharing the creative process with you and seeing all the fun stuff we cook up every week! Thanks to Paul, "The Egg Man," for proofreading this book and our blog. My grammar is equivalent to that of a fifth grader, but luckily Paul is verbally advantaged and cleans up my mess. Lots of folks ask me about my publisher and do I enjoy working with them. I can't say enough great things about Mango Publishing. They are so easy and professional to work with. If you are thinking about publishing a book, shoot them an email!

Thank you to the collaborative partners of FlavCity, it's a pleasure to recommend your best in class products to my community: Thrive Market, Celtic Sea Salt®, HighKey, Crepini®, Four Sigmatic, Meat & Livestock Australia, Coconut Secret, Siete, Native Forest, Hu Chocolate Gems, Rao's Homemade®, Lakanto, Primal Kitchen, Mighty Sesame Co, Sky Valley®, Mowi and Kettle & Fire.

BOBBY, FLAVCITY HAS EMPOWERED ME. I DON'T JUST BUY
GROCERIES THAT LOOK HEALTHY ANYMORE. I NOW KNOW
WHAT THINGS ARE HEALTHY THANKS TO YOUR CHANNEL. I
NEVER REALIZED HOW DECEIVING PACKAGED FOODS ARE
UNTIL YOU SCHOOLED ME. I DON'T EVEN PAY ATTENTION
TO ANY OF THE FLUFF ON FRONT. I TURN THE ITEM OVER
IMMEDIATELY. YOU HAVE REALLY MADE A DIFFERENCE
IN ME AND MY FAMILY'S QUALITY OF LIFE. THANK YOU!

–FREDERICK S.

ALLERGEN INDEX

RECIPE	PAGE	KETO	PALEO	VEGAN				
BREAKFAST ALL DAY								
MINI MEATBALL BREAKFAST HASH	37	✓	✓		✓		✓	
QUINOA BREAKFAST BOWL	38			✓	✓	✓	✓	
KETO TRUCKER'S BREAKFAST	41	✓	✓		✓		✓	
CRISPY CREPES BENEDICT	45	✓			✓			✓
POST-WORKOUT PROTEIN SMOOTHIE	46				✓	✓	✓	
NO-BAKE GRANOLA	51		✓	✓	✓	✓	✓	
BREAKFAST TACOS	54				✓		✓	
CARNIVORE STYLE								
TIKKA MASALA BEEF KEBABS	59	✓			✓	✓		✓
CRISPY SKIN LEMON CHICKEN	60	✓	✓		✓	✓		✓

RECIPE	PAGE	KETO	PALEO	VEGAN	Gluten-Free	Egg-Free	Dairy-Free	Nut-Free
BBQ BABY BACK RIBS	63					✓	✓	✓
CRUSTY LAMB CHOPS WITH GREEN TAHINI	66	✓	✓		✓	✓	✓	✓
GRILLED KOREAN SHORT RIBS	71				✓	✓	✓	
CHICKEN PESTO AND VEGGIES	72				✓	✓		
BEEF CHILI	75				✓	✓		✓

COMFORT FOOD

RECIPE	PAGE	KETO	PALEO	VEGAN	Gluten-Free	Egg-Free	Dairy-Free	Nut-Free
WILD MUSHROOM AND KALE TAGLIATELLE	79				✓			✓
FRIED WILD RICE AND CHICKEN	83				✓		✓	✓
RISOTTO-ISH	86				✓	✓		✓
CHICKEN ENCHILADAS	89				✓	✓		
SPAGHETTI CARBONARA	93				✓			✓
BEEF AND NOODLE STIR FRY	94				✓	✓	✓	✓
CAULIFLOWER MAC AND CHEESE	97				✓	✓		
KETO CAULIFLOWER MASH	100	✓			✓	✓		✓
HONEY GLAZED CARROTS	103		✓		✓	✓	✓	✓

DESSI'S PALEO SWEETS

RECIPE	PAGE	KETO	PALEO	VEGAN	Gluten-Free	Egg-Free	Dairy-Free	Nut-Free
BULGARIAN HONEY COOKIES	109		✓		✓		✓	
STICKY DATE PUDDING	113		✓		✓		✓	

RECIPE	PAGE	KETO	PALEO	VEGAN	🌾	🥚	🥛	🥜
BERRY PANNA COTTA	116		✓		✓	✓	✓	✓
CHOCOLATE CHIP COOKIES	119				✓			
LEMON OLIVE OIL CAKE	123		✓		✓		✓	
VANILLA CUSTARD WITH STRAWBERRY JAM	126		✓		✓		✓	✓
ORANGE AND CHERRY BISCOTTI	129		✓	✓	✓	✓	✓	
PEACH CRISP A LA MODE	132				✓	✓		
DOUBLE CHOCOLATE DATE BROWNIES	135		✓		✓		✓	
IMMUNE BOOSTING TEA	138	✓	✓		✓	✓	✓	✓
ITALIAN ALMOND COOKIES	141		✓		✓		✓	
CREAMY HOT COCOA	142		✓		✓	✓		✓
CHOCOLATE AVOCADO PUDDING	145		✓	✓	✓	✓	✓	✓
HAPPY HOUR								
CHEESEBURGER AND SWEET PATATO FRIES	149				✓			✓
SUGAR-FREE MARGARITAS	152	✓	✓	✓	✓	✓	✓	✓
CRISPY BAKED CHICKEN WINGS	155	✓			✓	✓		✓
CAULIFLOWER PAN PIZZA	158	✓			✓			✓
SUGAR-FREE LEMONADE	161	✓	✓	✓	✓	✓	✓	✓

RECIPE	PAGE	KETO	PALEO	VEGAN	Gluten-Free	Egg-Free	Dairy-Free	Nut-Free
HARISSA HUMMUS PLATTER	162				✓		✓	166
KALE AND CAULIFLOWER SALAD	166	✓			✓	✓		
BBQ PULLED PORK TAQUITOS	169		✓		✓	✓	✓	
BRAZILIAN CHEESY POPOVERS	173				✓			✓
ROASTED BEET HUMMUS	176		✓	✓	✓	✓	✓	✓
UNDER THE SEA-FOOD								
SWEET AND STICKY SHRIMP CAKES	180		✓		✓		✓	✓
SALMON COBB SALAD	183	✓	✓		✓		✓	✓
CRUNCHY SHRIMP TACOS	185		✓		✓	✓	✓	✓
SALMON PATTIES AND TARTAR SAUCE	189	✓	✓		✓		✓	
LAZY A$$ TUNA SALAD	190	✓	✓		✓		✓	✓
IT'S ALL ABOUT THAT BROTH								
RED THAI SCALLOP SOUP	195	✓	✓		✓	✓	✓	✓
LENTIL CURRY STEW	196				✓	✓	✓	✓
ITALIAN WEDDING SOUP	199				✓	✓	✓	✓
NOURISHING BEEF BONE BROTH	200	✓	✓		✓	✓	✓	✓

UNTIL I DISCOVERED BOBBY AND FLAVCITY I HADN'T

REALIZED HOW ADDITIVES WERE AFFECTING MY

HEALTH. NOW I CAN MAKE HEALTHY CHOICES AND

THE AMAZING RECIPES ARE SO TASTY. I FEEL WELL FED

AND SO MUCH BETTER. THANK YOU SO MUCH XX

–JACQUI G.

INDEX

Bobby, Dessi, and Rose live in Chicago, and you can follow their adventures by following @flavcity anywhere on social media. Bobby is usually at the grocery store, the gym, or in the kitchen cooking. Dessi loves to paint, but lately all of her time is spent raising Rose, baking paleo goodies, and building the new Bobby Approved shopping guide app.

To see more recipes and videos, make sure to subscribe to the *FlavCity* YouTube channel and follow FlavCity on Instagram, Facebook, and at www.flavcity.com.

Mango Publishing, established in 2014, publishes an eclectic list of books by diverse authors—both new and established voices—on topics ranging from business, personal growth, women's empowerment, LGBTQ studies, health, and spirituality to history, popular culture, time management, decluttering, lifestyle, mental wellness, aging, and sustainable living. We were recently named 2019 *and* 2020's #1 fastest-growing independent publisher by *Publishers Weekly*. Our success is driven by our main goal, which is to publish high-quality books that will entertain readers as well as make a positive difference in their lives.

Our readers are our most important resource; we value your input, suggestions, and ideas. We'd love to hear from you—after all, we are publishing books for you!

Please stay in touch with us and follow us at:

Facebook: Mango Publishing
Twitter: @MangoPublishing
Instagram: @MangoPublishing
LinkedIn: Mango Publishing
Pinterest: Mango Publishing
Newsletter: mangopublishinggroup.com/newsletter

Join us on Mango's journey to reinvent publishing, one book at a time